YOUR PERSONAL POWER PYRAMID

EDWIN CARPENTER

For Jordan, Brad, and Brian

You cannot choose your battlefield.

The Gods do that for you.

But you can plant a standard.

Where a standard never flew.

—Nathalia Crane

Table of Contents

Introduction

This book is the genesis of seventy-five years of life and of seventy-plus years of reading and writing, and my need to provide to our son, Jordan, his cousins, and now you, a simple yet powerful set of principles and reference points from which he could be successful. By successful, I do not measure success by money. By successful, I do not measure success by how handsome you are, how "in" you are, the size of your "McMansion," or other superficial measures. By successful, I mean the self-awareness of your own personal value and how, whatever way you choose to do so, you add value through the advancement of humankind. That is how humankind has evolved, and each of us has the duty to advance the standard.

Your Personal Power Pyramid is not a long book. It is just something that you can always have handy to refer to when in doubt or when you think you have lost your way. It is also, hopefully, the handy reminder that, as the Saturday Night Live comedian, Lillie Tomlin, observed, "Even if you win the rat race, in the end, you are still just a rat." It encourages you to rise above the battlefield, get out of being in the thick of things, and plan where you want your life to go. If nothing else, by rising above it, you may see your enemies better. But most of all, it suggests a higher human purpose than the "rat race."

As Jordan is aware, our family's life journey has not been without our own trials and tribulations. We have experienced the massive power of the United States Department of Justice. We know about the fairness of that system, including the Federal Court's criminal procedures. We also know that oftentimes, in that system, the process punishes one charged with a crime for exercising one's "constitutional" rights, and the charges alone cause the damage, even if one is innocent. In my case, the "justice" system was not about fairness or even moral righteousness. It was just a tool used by the federal prosecutors to silence me as a witness for my client. I have suggested that this was done out of fear of what I would say rather than crimes of opinion. The system was all about a war of attrition (who can last the longest) and little about innocence. In war, everything is "fair," including deceitfulness. Ultimately, I determined that it was in our family's best interest to end the struggle ("dive on the sword" as I have characterized it) and attend a federal prison camp for twenty-one months. In the process, though, we all learned a great deal. It is not the situation or circumstances you are in that define you; it is what you do about it. One biographical incident does not constitute one's destiny. Achievements or setbacks are but stepping-stones in your journey.

The goal here is not so much a book of knowledge or a book of motivation. Rather, it is a way of looking at things: at personal power. It is a summary of the development of my thoughts along life's journey so far. It is a foundation for going forward to consider and examine new experiences and novel ideas, and to examine them in a reflective manner.

I am hopeful that you will enjoy the short journey with me and take this pyramid of power with you wherever you go and with whatever your life's journey may hand to you. In life, we get what we are given, and we must decide what to do with it. Then we will always be together wherever we may be, in spirit, as it should be.

When Moses was alive, these pyramids

were a thousand years old.

Here began the history of architecture.

Here people learned to measure

time by calendar, to plot

the stars by astronomy.

And here they developed

the most awesome of ideas:

the idea of eternity.

—Walter Cronkite

Chapter 1
Why the Pyramid?

The central reference point of this manuscript is the pyramid. My focus is our son, Jordan, and his two cousins, Brad and Brian Thies; so this manuscript is directed to them.

The three of you are still young, and while you use metaphors all the time (the word "like" usually couples a concept with its reference point, such as "tastes like skunky beer"), it may be useful for us to consider what a metaphor is and how it is used in language to convey a concept. A metaphor is a figure of speech in which the term is transferred from the object it ordinarily designates to an object it may designate by comparison, such as the ship of life. Its purpose is to give you a reference point, a visual image of something that is intangible, to give it a physical form that one can relate to. It is a tool to assist in understanding.

Now, let me use a metaphor to assist you in understanding a metaphor. A metaphor is like a menu. The menu is a reference source for you at the restaurant. It assists you and gives you choices on what is available to eat. As a reference point, you can use it to decide what you will have for dinner.

Yet when you decide on the "prime rib" on page two of the menu, you do not eat page two of the menu, do you? You wait until the actual meal comes. In the case of the pyramid, there is no actual pyramid in your brain or in your diaphragm. It is a reference point to assist you in identifying the elements of power that you have within you to propel you to personal achievement. And you do not have to carry the actual pyramid with you to have the power of the reference point, nor do you need to consume the pyramid to acquire the power.

Now, why the pyramid?

The pyramid (particularly the Great Pyramid of Khufu (Cheops)) is believed to be the world's oldest stone structure. It is one of the seven wonders of the ancient world. Others were the Hanging Gardens of Babylon, the Temple of Deana at Ephesus, the Statue of Zeus at Olympia, the Mausoleum at Halicarnassus, the Colossus of Rhodes, and the Pharos of Alexandria. All are gone, except the many pyramids around the world. Yet the Great Pyramid is a unique structure. Some say it was built by the gods or even intelligent beings from outer space. What do you think? While not verified by me, here are some intriguing facts others have developed:

a) Is it a coincidence that the height of the Great Pyramid multiplied by a thousand million—98,000,000 miles—corresponds to approximately the distance between Earth and its Sun?

b) Is it a coincidence that the meridian that runs through the Great Pyramid divides the seven continents and oceans into two equal parts and lies in the center of gravity of the continents? Did the Egyptians even know the other continents existed or even what a continent is?

c) Is it a coincidence that the area of the base of the pyramid divided by twice its height gives us pi, the number that is used to find the area and circumference of pi, for circles?

d) Is it a coincidence that the pyramid is constructed on a virtually level rock base, even though its base is roughly two and one-half football fields on each side?

e) How could the engineers of Khufu know the spherical shape of the earth, the number or distribution of the seven continents, or the location, direction, or number of oceans?

f) With what technology was the rocky terrain leveled? What equipment was used? How did these engineers drive tunnels into solid rock that are smooth? How was construction illuminated? There were no torches found; there are no blackened ceilings or walls in the Great Pyramid.

g) How were stones weighing seventy tons cut out of quarries? How were these stones transported to the construction site and then joined so tightly together to be 1/1000 of an inch apart? How do seventy-ton blocks get raised up 300 feet into the structure?

h) It is estimated that there are 2,600,000 stone blocks in the Great Pyramid. It weighs an estimated 6,500,000 tons. Using engineering techniques of that time and 100,000 men, it has been estimated that it would take 600 years to construct the Great Pyramid. Yet it is said it was done in 20 years. How was that possible?

i) The position of the Great Pyramid and the other two pyramid structures mirror the positions of the three principal stars in the constellation Orion as it would have been located around 10,400 BC. Is this just a coincidence?

j) Is it a coincidence that the capstone of the Great Pyramid marks True North within 3/60 of a degree?

k) Is it a coincidence that the dimensions of the Great Pyramid give us other cardinal dimensions of the planet? For example, the height of the structure times 43,200 will give you the Polar radius of the planet. The perimeter of the base of the structure times the same 43,200 will give you the equatorial circumference of the planet. (There is relevance to the number 43,200, but that is for another day.)

l) As an engineer, to take on the construction, let alone the planetary relationships, must have been a massive feat indeed. Look how incredibly clever it was accomplished.

Suffice it to say, there are many other facets of the Great Pyramid's size, dimensions, and construction that make it difficult (if not improbable) for a critically thinking person to conclude that it was made by Egyptians. Yet it is believed to be the oldest and greatest existing monument to the power of humankind. The world has no other substantial physical and historical record of the efforts of humans before the pyramid (other than maybe Göbekli Tepe). There is no evidence that a true pyramid was ever built before by man prior to the erection of this magnificent structure. How did they do it? How did they know we had a planet?

It is grand and apparently indestructible as it stands. As a building, it stands at the head of the world in age, the vastness of dimensions, the perfection of workmanship, and the practical mastery of engineering feats and problems that are hard even for our modern engineering technology to grasp. It is a miracle in stone, as suggested in the Nineteenth century by Joseph Seiss, who wrote this wonderful book about pyramids.

When the Great Pyramid was constructed, who constructed it? I understand there is an ancient manuscript at the Bodleian Library at Oxford University in England. In that manuscript, the Copic author, Mas-Udi (also referred to as Masoudi), contends that the Egyptian King Surid had the pyramid built. History tells us that he ruled Egypt before the Great Flood. It is said in that manuscript that Surid had a premonition of the flood and instructed all of the priests to write down the sum total of all wisdom and conceal that wisdom in the Great Pyramid so that such wisdom would not be lost. There are many who contend that the Great Pyramid was built with divine intervention or that of extraterrestrial intelligence. But just consider that the Great Pyramid is a precise structure. The tiniest errors in measurements would result in not a pyramid at the top but sort of a corkscrew. This is space-age work. No one really knows.

I have never visited the Great Pyramids in Egypt. Maybe, someday, I will. But there are other examples of ancient structures much closer. For example, there is the Mayan pyramid in Cholula, Mexico, called Tipanipa. I understand that it is truly the largest pyramid in the world. Its base is 1476 feet by 1476 feet, and its height is 217 feet (Khufu is taller, however). Tipanipa is almost one-third larger than the Khufu structure, and it is arguably the largest monument ever constructed anywhere in the world. What is further interesting about Tipanipa is that in the sixteenth century AD, the Roman Catholics built a church on top of it because the site had sacred significance to the people of Cholula. The Catholic priests thought Tipanipa was just a great mound when, in reality, it was the largest pyramid ever constructed.

There are, of course, other examples of pyramids. There is the Mayan temple at Chichen Itza (that I have stood on top of) and the Aztec temple at Tenochtitlan. All are awesome and marvelous monuments created by humankind that have stood the test of time. Some are also reminders to us that humankind will be vicious to itself through human sacrifice in the name of its self-created "gods." Then there are those mediocre "knockoffs" of others that were called pyramids. The worst (best) example is that of the tomb of the Roman "noble," Gaius Cestius, in Rome. His claim to "pyramid fame" was that his pyramid was constructed in 330 days, and it shows. It is now part of the Aurelian Wall, an outer wall of Rome, next to the Protestant Cemetery. The Cestius pyramid, fabricated from ego, falls far short of those of the Egyptians and Mayans. It may have been a useful addition to the outer walls of Rome, but even the inner walls of Rome fell when the "barbarians" decided it was time for some old-fashioned, creative destruction. (Harsh it was, but necessary.)

There is an old Arab proverb: "Man fears time; yet time fears the pyramids." The pyramid is a powerful, visual tool as a reference point. It is a solid base to begin.

Finally, for easy access, if you need to refer to the pyramid to refresh your recollection as to your five components of personal power, just pull a one-dollar bill from your wallet. On the back, you will find another rendition of the pyramid. There is that power even in the "mighty" dollar.

Why a pyramid then? It is just a man-made mountain. Yet it cannot be blown over, can it? Its structure belies the possibility. It is virtually indestructible. It is divine. It is a marvel, a thing of beauty—the greatest and oldest stone structure that human beings have had their hands in the construction of any structure since before recorded history began. It is there to reinforce humankind's relationship with the physical world and its contact with the spiritual world. Why not use such a model to build your personal power base? Why not seek such perfection in the design, symmetry, and construction of your life? If it is truly the result of divine intervention or extraterrestrial intelligence, why not take some of that wisdom and power and let it be the metaphorical foundation for your own power base?

It seems to me that these ancient, sacred structures, built to last, would provide a simple and fitting reference point for considering how each human can actualize and realize his or her personal power. We are all spiritual people, and the essence of humankind comes from our individual and collective ability to get things done—to accomplish great things. It is with that reference point of the pyramid that we begin our journey into the great power within each of us. I hope that this journey will inspire you to accomplish great things in your own personal and powerful way.

Your personal power pyramid

Every great structure has four cornerstones that provide the base and foundation for its design. Those cornerstones hold it together. I suggest that your personal power pyramid should have such cornerstones. Since I am a strong believer in the principle that life is all about making A's, I thought it would be helpful to label those characteristics, those cornerstones, that hold the pyramid together with the use of some masterful and powerful A words. That is how the reference points have been identified and labeled as action, attitude, awareness, and alliances. Then, of course, there is the capstone. Carrying forward the A words, I suggest that the capstone is Affirmation. Here is what it might look like:

Your Personal Power Pyramid

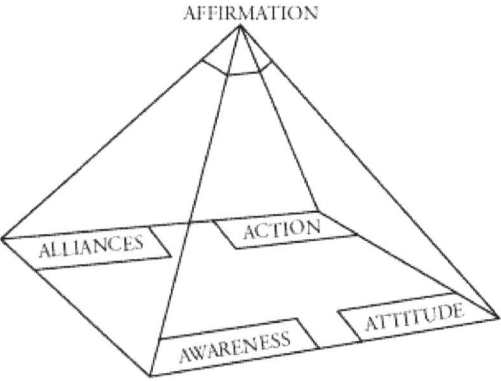

Let us begin.

ACTION

He who has begun is half done. Dare to be wise;
begin.

—Horace

Chapter 2
Your First Power: Action

When you think about it, all matter is made up of motion. Even atoms are mostly made of motion. Subatomic particles are made of motion—of energy. Nothing happens without motion. Nothing happens unless you act—get moving. This is a fundamental natural law. Action is the first cornerstone of personal power.

Action is about deeds done. You have heard me use the simple phrase: "Deeds are dear, and talk is cheap!" Action is the central theme in Nike's "Just do it!" Every day, you must get out there and do it. Think of it this way. The shepherd does not wait for the delinquent lambs to come home. If they do, they will soon be permanently missing one or more lambs and, eventually, the herd. Sheep don't come to the shepherd. The shepherd must go to the sheep. The flock is not there for the shepherd. The shepherd is there for the flock. (It is also a good object lesson in ego to consider the role of the shepherd. About the time you think you are great, consider that a dog can do the job better than you.) Jack Welch, the retired chairman of the Board of General Electric and probably the greatest success story in the last quarter of the twentieth century, put it this way:

Don't be paralyzed. Get energized.

Even the poster boy of simple-mindedness, Larry the Cable Guy, gets it when he pronounces the urgency of "Git 'r done!"

Certainly, there are obstacles to action. Obstacles are those events or things in life that obscure your view of the goals you have set. Tiger Woods' rough, if you will.

What kind of obstacles to action are there? Here are some examples for you to consider:

1. Resistance to change. This is clinging to the status quo, homo status, when we know that the old ways are gone, but we try to hang on, yet change is the universal constant of matter.

2. Waiting for something to happen. If I just wait long enough, someone will do it for me.

3. Feeling overwhelmed—paralyzed. I don't know where to start; not doing the things that need to be done to achieve positive results. This is the proverbial "deer in the headlights."

4. Time is not right. The conditions are never just right.

5. Self-doubt. I can't get it done. I don't want to lose. I'll just stay here, where I rationalize it is safe.

6. Adversity. I'm too discouraged to continue. I have been down so long; it looks like up to me.

7. Paralysis of analysis. Overanalysis of the problem.

If you want something to happen, you can't just think it. You must go do it. Make it happen. Ask for the order! Now, suppose you don't get the order. There is a natural law that always works in your favor. It's called the law of averages. For every action, there is a reaction. For every order you lose, you get one. But you have to ask for the order the next time. Great salesmen know this. You cannot stop moving.

The default mode of life

On the other hand, inaction leads to consequences by default, doesn't it? That is the world giving it to you, and you taking it. Whether you like it or not, the failure to act is a decision. Indecision becomes a decision by a mere lapse of time. If you wait for troubles to come to you, they will only multiply and build momentum against you during the wait. Waiting is a default mode, and experience tells me that the wait will only compound your problems.

Will Rogers once said this about action:

Even if you are on the right track, you'll eventually get run over if you just sit there.

If you are depressed, if you are paralyzed, how do you get rid of those feelings? It's simple: move it, and you'll lose it. It is not only what you do that you are accountable for, but also what you do not do. There are serious consequences to inaction.

The increment of better

One of the greatest secrets (maybe the greatest) in the world is this: You only need to be a small, measurable amount better than the other person (just a little bit above mediocre), and you will be successful. The word mediocrity has its source from Latin: "halfway up a stony mountain." Halfway up does not get to the top. It certainly doesn't put you at the bottom, but you may as well be at the bottom. If you cannot finish the mission, then you may as well not start it. But do not do it just because you were told to do it. Do it because you want to be of service. Do it because you want to contribute. Do it for yourself. You get back from the world what you put out there. When you put it out there, you will always get back more than you risk.

The Bible, as an ancient and sacred scripture, shows us the way in that regard. In Roman times, each Roman legionnaire had the right to demand that any civilian carry his pack one Roman mile (1,000 steps). From that came the phrase "Go the extra mile." What is its significance? When you go the extra mile, you are no longer a slave to the Roman. You are marching on your own terms. Now, the Roman dog must keep up with you. Besides, experience tells me that when you go the extra mile, it is truly a road less traveled. There is not much traffic, and the extra mile is the easiest mile you'll travel. There is no competition. There is no resistance, just the free-flowing advancement of your purpose. That is how to be effective—just being that little bit better will make you more than mediocre and will make you successful.

Decisions are not hard. It is the thinking about them that is the hard part. There is always a probability that the decision may be a poor one and that there could be adverse consequences. But you must do the best you can with the best information you have available to you. To worry about it puts obstacles in the way of clear thinking and decisive action. Dedicated, committed action on a sustained basis must be taken, even if you cannot control the result. The action alone will likely change the result.

Lastly, consider this. Change now comes at us at warp speed. The longer we wait, the more likely the opportunity will pass us by. Yes, there is much uncertainty in life. Particularly in this day and age, with change occurring at the speed of light, it is difficult to keep up with the knowledge and information that may be necessary to make good decisions. The fact is, however, that a good decision made now is better than a perfect decision later. In my judgment, the economic costs of delay will most often exceed the costs of a mistake. The mere lapse of time will change the whole dynamics of the perfect decision and make it not so perfect. Put another way, a good decision executed with dispatch always trumps a brilliant decision implemented slowly, without due regard to the consequences of delay. Your grandfather, "Pappy" Barr, said that he never made a bad decision. He took the best information he had and decided. Our friend Bill Wallace observed that perfection is often the enemy of success.

Why? The simple answer is that there is no answer book on certainty. First, small steps are always better than no steps. That is how you walk on the icy sidewalk, but you walk. Secondly, there is no upside to paralysis. If you don't move it, you lose it. Third, the law of averages always works with you when you take action. Behind every "no" is a "yes," but you will not find the "yes" if you stay where you are. You just remain in the "no" mode. The "no" mode is indecision. It is classic inaction.

Life is very much like fishing. This is always a great metaphor to work with. What is the most important element of fishing? You have to get moving and go where the fish are. You can't catch any fish if you are at home or just sitting at the marina. You won't catch every fish, but if you stop fishing, you won't catch any more fish either. Put your line back out there. Move to another spot. Change to a new lure. But if you go home and quit, there will be no more fish. No one catches any fish unless he or she is out there fishing. Going to where the fish are is more important than the most expensive bass boat, or the perfect lure, or the best bait. All of those will help, but these tools mean nothing unless you decide to take action and go where the fish are. Lastly, you must expect to catch a fish. No one rises from low expectations. You get what you expect, and if you expect no fish, then that is probably what you will get. Expect a boatload and plan for that result.

Your Personal Power Pyramid

The essence of the action is decision-making. In any situation, the decision is the fire to the fuse of action. It initiates the activity. Once committed, all sorts of wonderful things happen. Providence will provide you with what you need. It has always been so, but you have to take the first step. You have to take the leap of faith and hope that you will land on solid ground or, better, that you will learn to fly. But if you decide to do nothing, then there is no driving power—no intended purpose. As suggested earlier, there is a decision by default: consequences happening to you without your consent; without your input, you make yourself the victim. When you think about it, all action occurs twice. First, you consider what to do—you think; then, you do it.

You do not get your "should have" or "could have" in life. You only get what your "musts" are. You find a way to get it done.

Once the decision is made, you must be committed and stay the course, and you must be accountable for your actions. Equivocal commitment is the enemy. Without clarity of commitment, the gridlock of indecision will occur, and your cause may be lost.

Psychologists often suggest that we need to develop and use "commitment devices" such as written declarations or promises of commitments to a person or a cause. A good example is the Declaration of Independence. In business, we often have employees make written commitments to excellence or commitments to civility to define behavior. It then becomes easier to resist the "dark playgrounds" of temptation, absence of self-discipline, or maybe even the lack of belief in the future.

The inaction of worry

Worry is feeling anxious, uneasy, and troubled. Note that the action word in the definition is feel. To feel is an emotional response. While it may be a natural one, to face and conquer worry, one must get past the emotion and look for the etiology (the cause) of the feeling. Usually, worry is about some future event that the worrier thinks is going to occur that will be averse to some interest of the worrier. But we don't always worry about the future. Believe it or not, and silly as it may seem, we have feelings of anxiousness about—we continued to be troubled by—the past. We live in the present, so it is not likely that we worry much about the present. In the present tense, we have to go with the flow.

Now, the past is easy, don't you think? The past is fact. Specific circumstances came together at a particular time and at a particular place to produce a result—the result that was produced. It is a fact, not speculation. How can you be concerned or confused about the past? Maybe you should have a concern about what caused the result to happen. That is natural inquiry. You are a detective, looking for the cause. That is an investigation. That's not a worry. That is being proactive. You are not reacting to external stimuli. That is a healthy circumstance.

But if you really are worrying about the past, you must know that you are wasting your time. It has already happened, and you can't fix that event. It is not even likely that you can cover it up. (Sometimes, the cover-up is the greater "crime.")

What about the future, though? You are troubled by the uncertainty. You are paralyzed by the tasks that confront you. You know change is coming, and you don't want it to come. You don't know where to start. You don't want to fail, but you are concerned that you will not succeed. You are too discouraged to continue, but you worry about what the consequences will be if you give up. Does any of this sound familiar? It should. Those are all reactions to the uncertainty of change—the world's universal constant. The great Star Wars sage, Yoda, observed, "Impossible to predict, the future is." Impossible it is, indeed. So why engage in that exercise in futility?

Worry is that set of feelings that is part of the third stage of emotions arising from change and the grief process of letting go, accepting the past, and facing the future. Worry is confusion, the state of, as someone put it, "I am so confused; I don't know whether I've lost my horse or found a lead rope!" Your worry often was due to your estimation of it, not because of the circumstances themselves. The circumstance is or will be the circumstance. You may have little to say about it if it is the future, or you may have a lot. If it's the past, you have no further bearing on the subject. But you do have control over your estimate of it. You have the power to revoke or change any estimate. Worry does not exist, but your continued nurturing of it. It is like a baby; it grows larger by nursing it.

Someone once compared worry to the situation of paying interest on money you may never borrow and you may never owe. You wouldn't do that, would you? That is fiscally irresponsible. Worrying is psychologically irresponsible, isn't it?

Another appropriate metaphor for worry is that worrying is like being in a rocking chair. There is lots of motion, but you are not going anywhere.

Some people worry because something didn't happen when they wanted it to happen. So instead of a known, it remains an unknown. But God's delays, unlike justice delayed, are not God's denials. It will happen when it happens, and all of your worries will not make anything happen any sooner or later.

Many believe in divine order. It happened because that is what was intended to happen. You were blown off course because you were supposed to be blown where you are right now. This is not predestination because you have the power to rechart your course. That takes us to the heart of the problem. When you worry, it is because you are off course. There is only one way to stop worrying. Get busy. Start planning your routes. Adjust the rudder and the sails. Start figuring out how to get back on course; get busy fishing. It is only then that spirit comes to your rescue and helps you with the outcome. If you do nothing, it always results in consequences by default. Worry is emotion. It is not action. It is nothing. It moves nothing.

The principle of the bundle of sticks

Most of the worry is making something out of nothing. Your tasks overwhelm you. You don't know where to start. Here is a tool that I learned that will help you get started. It is called the principle of the bundle of sticks. It is the reverse of the old Aesop's Fable about the quarrelsome sons and the father's object lesson that a bundle of sticks held together cannot be broken. This is not a new idea, but it is a helpful reference point. Here is how it works:

Suppose all your problems are bundled together into a big stack— like a bundle of sticks. Then they are bound with worry. Altogether, you cannot break all those sticks at once, can you? But taking them one at a time, you can break them, and you can fuel your spiritual fire with them. Just release a little of that stranglehold on worry and pull one out. Focus on it and break it, then another, then another. Before long, the bindings are loose, and the bundle is smaller. Before long, all of those problems have been broken and consumed to make your spirit stronger. And the bindings of "worry" are gone.

How do you do that? You make a list, check it twice, and get busy. You make goals and write them down. You set priorities and try to meet them. If you don't get all of your tasks all finished today (and you never will until you die), make a new list tomorrow. Solve a few more problems. Before long, you have made the list smaller and more manageable. Before long, the stranglehold on your spirit is gone.

Worrying seldom lessens the burdens of tomorrow; yet worrying always saps the strength from the benefits of today. When you live in the present tense, you are dealing with it now. When you function in the present tense, there is no worry. There are problems to solve, goals to establish, issues to anticipate, people to see, and places to go. You are acting despite uncertainty, and you are clarifying the direction of your life. That is not worry. That is not paralyzing. That is an opportunity. No one ever complained about the want of opportunity. That is success.

Worry often manifests itself outward as one of the forms of anger (a particularly vexatious "A" word). If we feel inferior and worry that we will not be accepted by our peers, we may decide to force that acceptance on our peers. Anger is then just worry's big, bully brother. We also see worry manifesting itself as anger when others worry about us—particularly mothers worrying about their children. So when you see anger in others, you should naturally duck, but consider the potential source. It may not be worry, but usually the context of the anger can telegraph the source for you. If it is worry, maybe you can help yourself or the other person. If the anger is just the conduct of a bully, then avoid it.

Finally, experience tells me that most of the stuff we worry about never happens. If it does happen, it will not be because we duly deliberated in the "worry mode" about it, were anxious about it, or were anticipating that it would happen. It may happen, though, because you did nothing positive about it; you just worried about it. You were not proactive.

So we get results by default. Most of the bad stuff that really happens, we really don't worry about at all. It just happens. As our friend Michael Jamison observed, "Shit happens!" Most of the good stuff that really happens, we never did worry about. It comes from our efforts. Remember that worry is inaction.

The power of intelligent action: Goal setting and continuity

Do you know who a lackey is? A lackey is a follower. The word lackey comes from the word lack: a deficiency, an absence, without substance (or having very little of). The word has very negative connotations. It is a politically correct word for a "slave."

Contrast the image of the lackey with that of a leader. A leader is one who shows the way, the guide, the director of the course, the maker of the routes. Leadership is that state of being a leader.

There is much to work with from the view of the leader. Leaders always have a better perspective on life. They are either working from higher ground or leading the followers. Leaders don't eat much dust. There are no "rear ends" to obstruct the view. There is no walking in the offal of the rest of the herd. The scenery only changes for the lead dog.

To the leader, life is a blessing. To the lackey, life is a burden. Since you have the choice to be a lackey or a leader, what do you choose?

Even the cynical lawyer in Albert Camus's The Fall knew the difference between leader and lackey. He said leadership is solitary. On the other hand, slavery is collective. It's congregate—like the herd. He said slavery is the essence of the others getting theirs, too; at the same time, we get ours. That's what really counts to the herd mindset: All together at last, on our knees, our heads bowed, getting it hammered into all of us.

Again, contrast that view with the words of the Roman philosopher Epictetus, who discussed the essence of leadership. He said:

A true leader has the confidence to stand alone, the courage to make tough decisions, and the compassion to listen to the needs of others. He does not set out to be a leader, but becomes one by the quality of his actions and the integrity of his intent. In the end, leaders are much like eagles. They don't flock. You find them one at a time.

There is much difference in the essence, is there not? (Note the eagle reference, as well.)

Your Personal Power Pyramid

It is a far different thing to be passive. Peace, itself, is not passive. It takes hard work. That's why Jesus made one of the Beatitudes, "Blessed are the peacemakers." He didn't say blessed are passive, did he? But the most important peace you need to make is with yourself.

Let's look at leadership, now, from a personal perspective. If you lead your own life, then the model you create can be used by family, friends, and fellow human beings as a benchmark to aspire to. A metaphor might be helpful. Life is a ship. You are at the helm. Where is your ship going? You answer, "Nowhere, stupid, I'm sitting here worrying about that!" But while you are presently locked in the calm of uncertainty, that is temporary, isn't it? Your voyage of life is going somewhere, even if it's to the bottom of the ocean. Your job is to stay afloat and get out of the doldrums. Where are you going? Do you have a plan?

About 500 years ago, the French philosopher Montaigne observed:

No wind favors him who has no destined port.

Said another way, the author of the Peter Principle, Lawrence Peter, similarly suggested that if you don't know where you are going, when you get there, you will probably be somewhere else. All excellent performance starts with clear goals—a destined port. You must "Begin with the end in mind," as is suggested by Stephen Covey, a man a great deal wiser than me. To continue the sailing analogy further, I suggest that it is by the action of setting the sails, not the direction of the wind, that the destined port is reached.

All things are created mentally at first. You have a mental vision and purpose in the end result. If not, your ship will be sailing nowhere—stuck in the calm—or even worse, your ship may end up on the shoals of mediocrity.

What forms does leadership take? It is suggested that there are two fundamental elements. The first is setting goals. The second is following through, which I call continuity of direction.

To be effective, solution-directed, you must begin with an end in mind. Otherwise, you are just an efficient follower. There is a difference. Leadership is all about being effective. It is not about being efficient. Efficiency, you see, is about getting the job done right.

Effectiveness is about getting the right job done. Efficiency is about turning the crank the right way. Effectiveness is about turning the right crank.

Leadership is all about routes. It is effective. It sets the sails to determine the right route. Efficiency is making sure the planes and trains run on time. How about you? Are you doing the right things, or are you just doing what you are told to do (hopefully the right way)?

Within the context of your life, what are you doing? Have you been majoring in minor things? Most people are not lazy. They have just set for themselves relatively minor and unimportant goals. Their routes are unpowerful. From my experience, many prisoners follow similar curricula of life while in prison. (If one reviews such a prisoner's prior life, the pattern would probably be the same.) These men and women are masters of minutia, majoring in minor things. Consider these examples:

1. Some prisoners are memorizing all of the words to all of the songs ever sung by Shania Twain so that they can shine at karaoke when they are released.

2. Others spend every evening of every weekday in the weight room building their backs and arms so that they will be fully qualified ditch diggers when they are released.

3. Some prisoners sleep an extra eight hours a day, deluding themselves that they are getting extra good conduct time (EGCT) from the prison administration, resulting in either an earlier release or being fully qualified to be a subject in sleep disorder studies when they are released.

4. Others play pool or cards (or both) all night, every night, getting ready for the pro pool tournaments or the big stakes card games when they are released.

5. Many prisoners watch ESPN every day, every night, so that they can be qualified to be sports critics or color announcers when they are released.

You know the ones. You see them every day. They will be the ones criticizing the mirror for what they see when they are given their liberty, blaming their own incompetence on the system they were subjected to while in prison. Misery always loves company.

The great American architect Frank Lloyd Wright had a description for these people and their ilk. He would have compared them to his infamous Foo Foo Bird. Wright described the Foo Foo as that particular and special bird of mythology that always flew backward, not to keep the wind out of his eyes, but because it didn't care where it was going, and it had to see where it had been.

Even worse than unimportant goals is the person with no goals at all—having no intended purpose whatsoever. Such men and women either are in a state of constant depression or skitter here and there with no place to go. The latter are those that have what I call the Mad Hatter's condition. You may recall the Mad Hatter in Alice in Wonderland. He was wildly running from here to there, frantically reporting, "I'm late; I'm late, for a very important date!" But he never ever got there because he was always interrupted by some other tasks, always sidetracked, or derailed by some other issue. To use the ship metaphor, many of us are wildly following the many currents, winds of life, even currents they have consciously chosen, but none of which would lead them to any destined port—forever adrift. Even worse, they may be moving in ever-increasing speeds and ever-decreasing concentric circles until they end up on the ocean floor as a result of the whirlpool they have self-induced. Here is an example of the Mad Hatter's syndrome:

Early Saturday, I decided to get the car washed. As I left the kitchen, I decided to get a can of pop for the road. I went to the pantry, and the trash can was full. I stopped to dump the trash. As I reached for the new trash bag, I saw the bag of dog food and thought I could dump that into the dog food bin, so I took the bag. On the way to the bin to dump the dog food, I saw the mail on the kitchen table. I dropped the bag of dog food by the bin and took the mail toward the home office. I dropped the mail on the desk and saw that the water bill had not been paid and was overdue. I stopped to pay the bill since the mailbox was on the way to the car wash. But there were no checks in the checkbook, so I went to the cabinet to get a new book of checks. On the way, I noticed that although the television was turned off, the satellite dish was still on. I went looking for the remote. Then the telephone rang, so I stopped the search and got the phone. As I was talking to my neighbor, Mark, about a project at his house, I saw that the clock needed to be wound, so I stopped to do that. Just as I was about to wind the clock, I saw that a plant in the office looked wilted, so I went to the guest bathroom to get a pitcher of water. In the guest bathroom, I saw that there was no toilet paper in the holder. I looked in the cabinet for TP, and there was none, so I went to the utility room to get a package of toilet paper. On the way, I saw a load of wash that needed to be changed, so I stopped to change the load. Just as I was about to do that, I saw the satellite remote in the kitchen. What was it doing there? I remembered I was going to shut off the satellite, so I stopped what I was going to do and grabbed the remote. In doing so, I knocked over a glass of milk on the table, so I went to get a towel to clean up the mess.

And so on, it went—a flurry of constant activity, but nothing got done. At the end of the day, the car was still not washed. There were lots and lots of activities, but no firm results. Nothing really got accomplished.

Effort and activity do not equate to accomplishment. Your action must be directed to results—to closure. Being "worn out" does not mean that you got anything done—that you were successful at accomplishing your mission. Activity is not action. You are just moving molecules from one place to the next. Change without purpose. Action without an end. Always be mindful of the wisdom of Master Yoda, who observed, "Try or not try. There is no try. There is only do or not do!"

Plan your future. There is great power in planning, in goal setting. Goals create hope. They give inspiration—faith—to those adrift. Hope is not just a passion for the possible. With planning and goals, hope becomes a passion for what is promised. Promises fulfilled are powerful medicine, particularly if they are promises made to yourself.

Remember, it was not raining when Noah constructed the ark. It is always better to be prepared for the future (an opportunity or a crisis) and not have one materialize than to have a crisis or opportunity appear and not be prepared for it. Noah was prepared. The question is, will you be?

Goal setting is only half of the equation, though. So what if you have determined your destined ports? Have you ever learned to sail? Leaders not only set goals; they live those goals. They encourage and nurture their family members, friends, and fellow human beings to live those goals. Followers, on the other hand, don't care. They are rowing to be rowing—just taking orders (often all the way to the ocean floor). Leaders learn the difference between the goal of being a great human being and learning how to be a great human being. Having a goal and having lots of book learning about how to be is just an accumulation of information. You must do the next step. You must learn how to become, and you must teach yourself how to become a great sailor. You must teach others to be great sailors. You must do it to know it. You must execute the plan.

In sports, learning how is called practice. In the military, it's called drilling. Repetition is the mother of skill. The Greek philosopher Aristotle knew the power of practice. He said:

Excellence is an art won by training and habituation. We are what we repeatedly do. Excellence then is not an act, but a habit.

Sophocles put it another way. He said:

For though you think you know it, you can have no certainty until you do it.

Edwin Carpenter

Football coach Don Shula observed:

> Your game is only as good as your practice.

The Roman historian Josephus said this about the strength of the Roman legions:

> Their drills are bloodless battles. Their battles are bloody drills.

Or as John Wooden would instruct:

> Failure to prepare is preparing for failure.

You must learn to be a sailor; otherwise, you will never have the courage to leave sight of the shore. It has been said that smooth seas do not make for skillful sailors. When you learn to sail, you do not fear the storms of life. They are just on-the-job training. You should know by now that the winds of change are out there. Storms happen. The wind does change. You are misdirected by the current. How do great sailors handle those matters? Along with practice, you receive the traits of vigilance and focus, both of which help you keep your ship on course.

Having practiced, captains know they must be at the helm every day. Someone must be watching, checking daily to see if the ship is still on course. These captains don't take things for granted. They pay attention to detail. They are never complacent. They practice their trade, being the captain of their ship. When blown off course, they adjust the rudder; they realign the sails. They consult their maps and charts. They use the ship's various tools to help them stay on course. They take measurements to see where they are. They consult the ship's logs to see where they have been, and they review the maps and charts to plot and replot where they are determined to go. These brave captains are vigilant, and they stay focused on the task at hand. These captains follow through to meet their goals.

Leaders do what they say they are going to do. They always keep their promises. Daily action results in a successful voyage, a promise fulfilled, a commitment honored. In return, these captains gain control over their lives, and they empower others to take responsibility for their lives. In the end, all working together have the satisfaction of a voyage undertaken and well done. Do not forget, ever, that to become a great leader, you must have been first a great servant and learned how to serve—you've learned how to sail.

Captains also work smart. They know that sails work best when they follow the wind, not fight the wind. They know that routes work best that follow the currents. They learn to go with the flow. They do not work in a frenzy; they work with intelligence and intended purpose. They remain calm in the face of uncertainty and adversity.

Here is a parable that will help you know the difference between working hard and working smart. There is a story about the Tao master who taught his students goal setting and the importance of continuity of direction. A student of the master had set the goal of learning to walk on water so that he would walk on water across the river to get to the city across the way. The student practiced and practiced until he could. When the student had fully mastered the art

36

of walking on water, he brought his master to the river and said, "I can walk on water, Master. See that city across the river? I can walk across the river and go there. I have overcome!" The old master simply looked at the student and asked, "Why did you not just take the boat?" While the effort was inspiring, the student had missed the boat. The aim was to get there as practically as possible.

The psychologist Abraham Maslow used a lot of carpenter metaphors to explain things. He said this about those who are fanatical about their efforts:

> The carpenter is not the best who makes more chips than all the rest.

(This is Mad Hatter syndrome.)

Maslow also observed:

> When the only tool you own is a hammer, all problems begin to resemble a nail.

Great sailors have many tools. They have sails (large and small), compasses, sextants, charts, logs, maps, and a rudder. They stay focused, and they remain vigilant; they methodically stay on course. And they do not set foolish routes against the wind or the current. Lastly, they practice every day. Those traits are called continuity of direction—following through with the plan to get to the destined port.

Your Personal Power Pyramid

It is by setting goals and continuity of direction that we create purpose in our lives. The purpose is to train yourself and your family members, friends, and fellow human beings to be the best crew you can assemble. Then no one ends up at the bottom of the ocean. Look at it this way. Life is the sum total of many successful years. Successful years are the sum total of many successful months. Successful months are the sum total of many successful weeks. Successful weeks are the sum total of many successful days. Successful days are the sum total of many successful hours. That is why practicing successful habits is the most certain way to meet your goals.

Don't be misled, however. Life is not easy. Setting goals and following through is hard work. Even if you do your best, you won't always get there. There is risk in life. There are obstacles. But when you take your eyes off the goals and focus on the obstacles that obscure your vision, then you get lost in the fray. As they said during the Vietnam War, "…You are up to your ass in alligators."

Procrastination

Procrastination, putting off to tomorrow, is the greatest killer of positive action. It is a persistent act of ruining your whole life for no apparent reason. Not doing what must be done today only adds to your responsibilities tomorrow. Very much like with "worry," nothing gets done. My father, "Big Al," was a master at this—sort of a master of productive disaster, if you will. In my judgment, procrastination should be synonymous with mediocrity. Each of us only has so much time, and each of us has the same amount every day. We all start out on an equal level playing field with time. If we do not use it (time) wisely, every day, we lose it. It is as simple as that. The trick, of course, is using time wisely. If we are honest with ourselves and are proactive, then there is no procrastination. Lincoln once observed that time is the silent artillery doing its destructive work while we are not engaged in the battle.

This is not to say that there should not be balance in your life. You do not need to work twenty hours a day. You do not need to check your emails 24/7. There must be time for sleep; there must be time for play. The key for me is to decide each day what can be eliminated (what I really don't need to do) and what can be delegated so that I can concentrate on what I want to do and what I believe will be the best return on time invested. Someone wiser than me suggested that leveraging time is like compounded interest in your bank account. Is that not a better plan than "worry" or "mediocrity," which may be paying interest on a debt you do not owe?

Some thoughts about character may be appropriate here. Whether you recognize it or not, character comes from harsh lessons in the seas of uncertainty. Character does not come from sunshine and roses. Each harsh lesson strengthens your resolve; it makes you fit for greatness. Character is forged from fire, force, and friction. It is made like a sword—between hammer and anvil, with heat and with a whetstone. If you do not heat it, if you do not pound it, it will be brittle. It will break. If you do not sharpen it with friction, it will be dull. It cannot cut. Likewise, take the pressure off the coal, and you will have no diamond. Take the irritating sand out of the oyster, and there will be no pearl. Such is the nature of life.

The captain has character. He has been there in times of storm. He mans the helm in times of trouble. He teaches his crew to manage the storms of life. The lackey always goes below. The captain of the ship is chosen from those with experience and expertise in sailing. The captain is not chosen from the passengers who are the best looking, have a pedigree, and have the best upbringing. You must never forget that those who stay on deck always get to see the rainbow at the end of the storm—the splendid gift for the survivor. All storms pass. They do not last. Experienced sailors do! Dare to begin every day, set your direction, and get busy sailing.

It also seems appropriate here to talk a bit about what character is and isn't. Lincoln once observed that character is like a tree. The roots of character come from having a solid foundation to grow from. Character is what you are made of, and those strengths are deeply embedded within you.

You should always be mindful of the distinction between character and reputation. They are two entirely different things. Character comes from within you—an inside job, much like happiness. It is what you decide to make of yourself. Reputation is what others think of you. Character and reputation do not always mirror themselves. Reputation is the shadow cast by the tree of character, but it is not the same. The important element is what you decide to make of yourself.

This whole principle of action comes down to this, in my judgment. Commitment and results are far more important than all the talk in the world. Chief Joseph once observed that good words mean nothing unless you do something about them. Doing something about it always starts with the first step and ends with the last. But the first step is always the quantum leap in my judgment. The German philosopher Goethe said it this way in one of his couplets:

Whatever you can do,
Or dream that you can do,
Begin in boldness.
Boldness has genius, power,
And magic in it.

In its simplistic form, it is the "I do!" plan of life. Get in. Get it done. And then get out and play! That is how you get results. You must learn to set your goals and execute them to be successful.

Experience tells me that your quality of life comes from the ability to control one's emotions and be habitual about that control. Pain is a fact, but suffering is an emotion. It is a choice.

The country singer Mitchell Tenpenny, in his song "Bucket List," observes that life is like your first kiss. You never know how long it will last. You always get what you get busy and get. Make good use of your life.

Your first cornerstone is action.

ATTITUDE

Your living is determined not so much by what life brings to you as by the attitude you bring to life.

—John Homer Mills

Chapter 3
Your Second Power: Attitude

Attitude is one of the five essential traits of personal power. What is attitude? It is your mindset. It is your state of mind. It is your demeanor: how you carry yourself, how you position your body, how you view things, and how you think about things.

Have you ever seen someone in a depressed condition? He or she is usually sitting or lying down, inert, almost in a fetal position. If the depressed person is standing, his or her posture will be deplorable. This person will be slump-shouldered, looking at dirt, and kicking rocks on the road of life. How far will this person get in the foot race of life? Even if on the right road, do you think he or she is at risk of getting run over, as Will Rogers observed?

How do you get rid of—get out of—the state of depression? You change your state. Change your physical state, and you change your attitude—you change your state. It has been said that Zig Ziglar observed this about the importance of attitude:

> It's not your aptitude but your attitude that
> determines your altitude.

What is more important? Someone wiser than me once asked, "Is it your intelligence quotient (your IQ), or is it the 'I will' or 'I can' quotient that is more important?" You be the judge. Even if you are the smartest person in the world, if you believe you will fail, you will. If you believe you will succeed, you will. You will not get what you do not expect to get. The great psychiatrist Karl Menninger said it this way:

Attitude is more important than facts.

Viktor Frankl's view was that if you had a purpose, you could tolerate anything sent your way. Moreover, he said that you have the ability to control your attitude under any given set of circumstances. You have that choice every day. Put another way:

You can fill your day with pain, or you can fill your day with gain.

The choice is yours. Each day is the same. Each day comes one day at a time. Each day, you have the choice. What will it be? Pain? Or gain?

Every day, we are faced with potential or actual physical or financial adversity. Every day, we deal with toxic human beings—those with a bad attitude. Every day, we are subjected to the circumstances of our environment. But all of these things are outside of us. The question is whether we can manage our own internal thermostat—the choice of attitude.

Let me give you another example. Once (this happens often in the scheme of a traveler's life), I was on an airplane on my way to Miami, Florida, to give a speech at a convention. We flew through and around and over and under this massive storm on our way from Kansas City to Miami. The ride was less than pleasant. When we landed in Miami and went to the luggage carousel, we waited and waited and waited for our luggage. We were beaten up by the travel. All of us had developed a classic poor attitude. And just as you might have foreseen, when the luggage arrived, there were about thirty of us who received nothing. Apparently, our luggage had been lost or misplaced. Then, poor attitudes were transformed into anger as we all worried about our "stuff."

At that point, I decided that if I could laugh at it later, I could certainly laugh at it now. What was the point in being mad? The fact of the matter was that the airline personnel at the terminal had not lost (or misplaced) my luggage. They were just the messengers. So I decided to start sharing the absurdity of lost luggage with my fellow passengers. How could it be that luggage gets lost on a direct flight? Did they need my jammies that bad?

Soon, we were all joking about the situation and not agonizing about it. Our whole attitude had changed. Our whole view of the situation had changed. We were all sharing the misery of air travel, and then the misery was gone. Besides, we could not control it anyway. Our luggage was somewhere else as if it had a destination and a mind of its own.

As we all were then joking and laughing, patiently waiting in line to report our claim to the airline God of Lost Luggage, one of the baggage men came up and reported that our luggage had been found. One whole cart of luggage from our airplane had been erroneously sent to another airplane. Thankfully, someone had caught the error in time. Shortly, our luggage was rolling along the carousel, and we were on our journey.

See what I mean? Pain to gain! Luggage delayed was not luggage denied. Everyone tolerated the situation much better, all because we decided we could. The choice is always there. You just must recognize the opportunity for gain and seize upon it.

The second example is that of swimming lessons. Jordan may not remember this, but it really happened to him when he was small. Ginger had taken Jordan to the swim instructor, and during a lesson, he unsuccessfully tried to breathe some pool water. That obviously did not work well. He started choking. He started crying. He was afraid of the water. His swimming teacher then changed the way he should look at it. She made a joke out of it. She asked him why he was trying to swallow all the water in the pool. She suggested that if he was thirsty, she could get him a cup. Tears turned to surprise. Then the absurdity came out. Jordan started laughing, and soon he was back trying to float and even swim. His whole attitude changed from fear to fun. And he was prepared to learn, no longer worrying about choking or being fearful of drowning. All of that came from turning the tables on his attitude toward the matter. The choice is always there. Do not let the external keep you from the fun of life.

Lastly, consider this about attitude. Be thankful for what you have. Be thankful for what you can control. That has been called the attitude of gratitude. When you are in a positive attitude, it's infectious, and it's contagious—it rubs off on all those around you. It rubs them the right way, so to speak. Soon, all who are around you are pulling together for what is important, what is good for the group. And don't get sidetracked by obstacles or inconveniences. Never let your problems become excuses. Never believe in hurt or pain. Do not ever let a bad experience in the past shape your future. You have the power to influence the future—choose gain!

How we look at change

As you know, I spent some quality time in federal prison at the great expense of my family and society in general. Who would disagree that a change of accommodations from home to jail is a massive change in a person's life? It is the worst kind of change. It is a change imposed. And change imposed always meets with resistance.

Here is what I came to understand. The more pernicious effects of such changes are felt by my family. That change was more serious and more devastating than the change I was experiencing. If you think about it, you know it is. They have to face the community, family, and friends and have to explain to all of these interested persons. So while I thought my life was changing, guess what? To my family, my change of accommodations was the San Francisco earthquake, the Chicago fire, Hurricane Katrina, Black Tuesday, and the Day of Infamy all rolled into one. And they were on the scene of the disaster, not me. It is important how you deal with change in every context. My change was minor compared to theirs.

How you handle change affects not only your continued well-being but also the well-being of those around you. If you resist, instead of learning to go with the flow, you only make it more difficult for yourself and everyone else. At the same time, resistance to change makes it doubly more difficult for those who are important to you. Consider just this one example that I saw every day at camp. Suppose a camper plays tough guy. As a result, he ends up in solitary confinement with no contact with the outside world. No contact with his family means uncertainty. No contact means anxiety. No contact means fear. No contact means worry. Yet there is absolutely nothing his family can do about it—risk without any control. That is the worst kind of concern.

There he is, though—Mr. Tough Guy! He is showing no fear. Who is being hurt in this situation? I can tell you that it does not pain the prison guards at all. This is job security to them. But the situation does hurt his family. So whatever may happen, he cannot change it. Get over it. Get along with it. Get past it.

Beyond the injury to his family from macho conduct, consider this. Resistance to change, the nonacceptance of his circumstances, is juvenile. Children hate change. They want everything to stay the same. They want macaroni and cheese every night. God forbid, they want any peas. When the family needs to move, children do not want to move. Can't you hear it now: "We're not moving. We're staying here."

Guess what? Change means movement. Change results in friction. While it may be human to stick with what is known, what we get is daily doses of the unknown. With those doses come side effects—at best, inconvenience and at worst, outright pain. Yet what is the most universal constant? Change. There is nothing quite as sure as change, is there? What you do about it is what makes the difference.

Change really is about your perception of those external events around you. It is not really about those events. What it is really about is what you make of those events internally—how you deal with those events.

John F. Kennedy wrote, "Change is the law of life. Those who look only to the past are certain to miss the future." So while you are resisting, think about this. You are getting what you are getting because you are doing what you are doing. If you don't like what you are getting, then you change what you are doing. Then what you are getting will change, too.

Kennedy also told the story of the Chinese alphabet character for "crisis." It is two symbols. The first symbol is danger. But the second symbol is opportunity. You see, in life, you will come upon a whole series of opportunities masterfully disguised as problems or miseries. Opportunity is seldom labeled. But if you understand that change in external events, then you have the opportunity to make the change something positive, something better. When one door of life closes, another door always opens. The question is, will you see it? If you are busy trying to reopen the door that closed or gazing longingly at what is gone, you will miss the new door opening.

In the context of most situations, however, dealing with change always works better with allies. Who better to be your allies than your spouse and your children? Change is exchange. Start talking about it. Experience tells us that what you will gain will be better than what you gave up. You can never go back. You must go forward. You must end up somewhere else.

The greatest change that anyone faces is the death of a loved one—the loss of a loved one. Psychologists counsel us on the stages of death (loss). Those natural stages are denial, anger (arising from uncertainty, worry, confusion, depression), remorse (wishing you had spent more time, done this, had not yelled at, etc.), and finally acceptance. The same is true with any major negative event in your life. You will go through those natural stages, including the phase of Why me? You must remember, though, that each stage may not be long. You may get to acceptance quickly. But the sooner you get there, the better.

What is acceptance? How do you know you have arrived? Acceptance is the recognition that whatever has happened in the past, you cannot do anything about it. Not even God can undo the past. When you accept, you acknowledge and understand that specific circumstances of time and place have come together to produce the result they produced. It is nothing more, nothing less.

Once you accept them, you and your family can get along with the business of the future. The great news is that today could be the first day of the rest of your positive life. The further news is that the future comes one day at a time, starting now, if you let it.

Here is some wee wisdom from Dolly, the little girl in Family Circle, to her brother, Billy. Through Bil Keane, the artist, she conveys this message about the importance of today. Here is Dolly's explanation:

> Yesterday is the past. Tomorrow is the future, but
> today is a gift. That is why it is called the present.

The same can be said about worry. When you are in the present, learning how to sail, there is no worry, only action.

Be a change agent

For one to effectively respond to change—external events that cause an upheaval in one's normal patterns of life—it is necessary for one to recognize what needs to be changed. The transformation must be to oneself before anything else will change. This is the premise upon which all progress is based. Change yourself and how you look at it, and the world changes as well.

You must be willing to endure whatever events or circumstances come your way. Once you accept that as given, then you are freed to pursue higher purposes. Such purposes, if properly considered, can be moral and ethical purposes that lead to principled behavior and honorable conduct. Such purposes, if properly considered, will also be purposes that seek to move the social system in which you live into a higher level of development, a higher level of cooperation, an improved level of productivity. (Evolution?) Such purposes require you to be selflessly motivated—to be trusting. You must seek to advance the collective goals of those who trust you as well as your own.

Henry David Thoreau said:

> Action from principle, the perception and performance of right, changes things and relationships; it is essentially revolutionary and does not consist wholly with anything that was. It not only divides states and churches; aye, it dividesthe individual, separating the diabolical in him from the divine. (Emphasis supplied)

To be a change agent in your life and the lives of those you love, you must ask and answer some tough questions. You must ask yourself, "What is the right thing to do? How do I act in a more genuine way?" Then you must set out every day to answer those questions by your own conduct, your own actions. In that way, you set the example. You create the standard to which other human beings may relate. You are the agent of change. You set the benchmark for the conduct of others. What you soon find is that without you, in your absence, the system and its relationships aspire to meet or exceed that benchmark. Others become self-empowered, self-actuated, from the standard you have shown them.

On the other hand, suppose you elect to view your situation as hopeless. Others will aspire to that benchmark as well. They will have weak purposes, and theirs will be unprincipled behavior; theirs will be dishonorable action. They will become disingenuous, too. Such behavior will manifest itself in further conflict with authority, destruction of relationships, and emotional entropy. In both instances, such actions occur because the person (it could be you) has become disempowered. In many instances, however, disempowered people do not lose their creativity. Instead, that creativity is channeled (misdirected, rerouted) to sabotage themselves, their relationships, and the organizations in which they function.

To be a change agent, you must self-empower your own purposes. Whatever you may or may not have done in your life (be it good or bad) uniquely positions you in this time and place to achieve a wonderful and powerful mission in life. It is up to you, though, to ask the hard questions and answer them honestly. Make no mistake. How you see the world and how you act on it are translated into the behavior of others who surround you and interact with you.

Consider this, however. No punishment that any third party, no externality, or other factors can lay upon you could ever compare to the punishment you place on yourself by working toward your own diminishment. There's nothing at all. Unfortunately, you don't have to do much to get there. Entropy is the default state of things. Do nothing, and you get nothing in return. Certainly, there is order. Everything is in its rightful place. Incremental, ordered mediocrity is what you will have caused to be created by default. Do not forget that pain is temporary, but the will to win is forever. Success comes only from sacrifice.

Fear, someone once said, is an acronym. It is false evidence appearing real. Fear is an emotion. It is not a fact. Fear is paralysis. But deep down inside, I wonder whether our deepest, darkest fear is that we are powerful well beyond our perceived limitations. If we have unlimited power, then what happens if we fail? Our self-imposed limits become our safety net. We are safe within our box; we think we are secure. Besides, what would others think? If you believe you can do it, you can. In the scheme of things, how do you believe that playing small, selling yourself short, serves you or the world well? Do not fear your greatness. Liberated from your own self-imposed limitations, you become a positive example for others. Your mere presence liberates others. You can be the ebb tide and lower all boats, or you can be the high tide and raise all boats. The choice is yours. Would you prefer to be sucked down with all the rest or be the high tide and raise everyone else up? I know what I choose to do.

Whatever you expect out of life, you will get. Life is not a trial. It is not a challenge. Those are negative connotations. Life is all about you. It is you who brings meaning to your life. You decide what meaning your life is to have. No one else makes that decision. When you do bring meaning to your life, you bring meaning to the lives of others. Get busy. Act. Be an agent of change. I can tell you that no one rises from low expectations, no one. You will become what you aspire to be. But if you think less of yourself, the world will accommodate you. When you set a low value for yourself, the world will take the lower price and not bid against itself.

This insight comes from John Harricharan, a particularly insightful man:

> Life is lived from within, and no one can be hurt by what appears to be happening outside. You can change circumstances if you desire. Your only purpose in life is to make choices. Once the choice is made, the entire universe moves to fruition that which you choose.

Most of life is an inside job. You make of it what you want to make of it; you make of it what you do about it.

Finally, I want to share with you some wisdom from Pappy Barr, your grandfather, who once told me, "If you can't change it, you must change the way you look at it." We were discussing that issue in the context of death. The important thing about death is the life that was lived. We all need to look at that life and rejoice that it happened, rather than agonize over the loss. Similarly, when something happens to you, it happened. You cannot change that. It is history. But you can change how you look at it and what you are going to do about it. Do you want to be paralyzed, or do you want to get energized? The choice is always there. Every day, you get to decide whether to fill the day with pain or gain.

The inner thermostat of self-control

In life, if you let what happens to you get control over you, then you will always be responding to those outside stimuli. It is only too hot or too cold, based upon your estimate of it, not usually because of being too hot or too cold. You have the power to reject the effect of those external stimuli upon you. It is like trying to control the weather. What you can control, though, is your view of things affecting you and how you measure the effect of those things upon you.

Shame and humiliation come in many flavors. Shame comes from parents who want to control you. Shame comes from fellow human beings who want to shed their own shame and have you share theirs. Shame comes from the invasion of our bodies. Shame comes from irritable teachers, preachers, and bureaucrats. Shame comes from heritage or geographical origin. Shame manifests because a spouse wants to divorce you. Shame occurs because your child does not want you as a father or mother anymore. And shame comes in a thousand other flavors. Yet who is doing what to whom? The actions or words of others are exterior; it is how you read each of them that causes you shame or humiliation. Shame is a feeling, an emotion: it is not fact. It is fantasy. That shame or humiliation is self-fabricated, invented in your mind, your psyche, and it is always self-inflicted. It is the product of your emotions. Why apologize for something done to you? Why not put it behind you and get your sails readjusted?

The two monks

I once read this story. It is attributed to Irmgard Schloegel, from one of Jack Canfield's Chicken Soup for the Soul anthologies, and recharacterized by me. There once were two monks whose sect prohibited the touching of a female. Those two monks were journeying home to the monastery when they reached a rain-swollen river. Beside the river was an elderly woman who could not cross the river because she was frail and because she had a large bundle of possessions that burdened her ability to cross safely.

Upon reaching the old woman, one of the monks promptly put her on his back and carried her across the river. The other, while distressed at the sin of his brother, picked up the woman's possessions and carried them across, as well. When the first monk reached the other side, he sat the woman down and waited until the other arrived with her belongings. Then the two monks continued on their journey back to the monastery. For the longest time, the monk who had not sinned refused to speak. Finally, the sinner asked, "Why are you so silent?" The other answered, "You touched a woman!"

The sinner responded, "Yes, and I left her at the side of the stream. You are still carrying her? Why?"

Whatever may happen to you, whatever you have done—and it is done—you must leave it behind at the other side of the river. Do not continue to carry such heavy loads. You are not a beast of burden. You are a child of spirit. Get over it, dump it, and get along with your journey.

Never forget that you are somebody. The spirit never takes time to make a "nobody." The spirit doesn't make junk. You may turn yourself into junk. Worth is relative. Self-worth is not. Do not surrender your life to outside forces.

So what can you control, you ask? It is suggested that there are two things you can control. The first is your own excellence. Every day, you can be determined to do your best. When you do, you are competing not against the others, not against the ex-spouse, not against the money changers, not against ex-friends. Instead, you are competing against yourself. Your game is self-improvement. That game is never over until you stop breathing. In this game, you never lose; you always win. Do not let the lack of resources available to you stop you from acting. Resourcefulness is a great deal more important than resources made available to you.

The second thing you control is your own attitude under any given set of circumstances. You can change (transform) any set of circumstances into positive ones if you will it to be. Recall the stories of Frankl in the Nazi death camps. Even faced with death, there were those out there every day encouraging and empowering others to be survivors, as well. They were the ones smiling in the face of destruction. Many of those positive people survived.

We get what we are given in life. All events, circumstances, or situations in life have a positive or negative perspective. Each of us can choose to see the positive or the negative of that event. Whatever way you choose, you will be right. It is just that the consequences will be different.

If you see yourself as a failure, you will be one. If you teach your children that you are a loser, they will believe you. You get what you are getting until you change it. As Rev. Robert Schuller says, "The 'me' you see is the 'me' you'll be." Be a survivor, not a victim. Volunteer to be a survivor today. Don't volunteer to be a victim. That you control. It is your choice.

Willingness to contribute

Attitude oftentimes is merely about one's willingness to contribute to the good of the cause. The intended purpose is the goal. Your ability or inability, your knowledge or experience, your whatever, is usually less important than your resolve to contribute. What is important is your availability. "I can" is a great deal more important than any other element of motivation. In any situation, you bring an invaluable resource to the purpose of the mission—your ability to contribute however you can. It is attitude that counts. It is attitude that always trumps knowledge or wisdom. Unless you do something with it, knowledge and wisdom are but unread books in the library.

The attitude of laughter

Laughter is always a great attitude adjuster. Even in the darkest hour, even when you are sharing great sadness with others, if you maintain a positive attitude, your whole circumstances will change for the better. Tough times do not last; they always pass. And if you can look back at it and laugh, you may as well laugh about your current circumstances starting now.

Laughter will also break up the stress of life, of negotiations, of test-taking, or of whatever you may be burdened with at the time. Murphy's law (If there is more than one possible outcome of a job or a task and one of those outcomes will result in disaster or an undesirable consequence, then someone will do it that way.) and all of its corollaries apply to whatever you are doing, or others are doing. For some reason, probably because we are human, we will often outsmart ourselves and have the proverbial egg all over our faces. About the time you start believing that your plan is "fool-proof," you will be right. The plan will prove that you are the fool, so to speak. So why not laugh about it? There is a lot of poop out there; therefore, be the best pooper scooper you can be. Besides, it is great job security to know that improving the level of ha ha in your life can and will improve the lives of everyone around you. Laughter is contagious. Get laughing and get moving, and all will be well again.

Laughing at yourself and your circumstances, whether created by you or by external factors, also makes you humble. It demonstrates that you are not in control all of the time. Experience tells me that often those catastrophic events in life are there partly to remind us that we are not in control; rather, we are just on the journey. They remove us from self-centeredness to spirit-centeredness—a higher level of awareness. Your ego is not so important anymore. That can only be a good thing. When you commit yourself to the principle of contribution to the advancement of yourself and society, to serve, then you are part of the solution, not part of the problem. Sometimes, it is enough to just laugh about it. Get laughing and get on living.

Your second cornerstone is attitude.

Semper aude. (Dare to know.)

—Immanuel Kant

Chapter 4
Your Third Power: Awareness

I once gave a speech wherein I tried to impart to my audience the sources of external power. The speech was done for the purpose of demonstrating to the group that we all have within us the power equalizers, knowledge, and wisdom, if we will develop the resource. In that speech, I proposed, for hypothetical and discussion purposes, that there were three sources of external power—of forcefulness to get what we want. The three sources of power that were suggested were physical strength or force, wealth, and knowledge.

First, let us consider force. We all have been on the receiving end of that in our lives. Some of us may have even personified such physical strength as children, adolescents, or even adults. It is the power to take from others by physical aggression; it is the playground bully, the street corner "gangbanger," the Mafia seller of protection (usually from that bully, himself). The Romans had a name for this source of power, as they taught logic to their students—ad baculum. It is a resort to the stick.

Second, I suggested that wealth was an external source of power. Wealth buys what it needs, whether it be bullies, tools, or those with other wisdom or influence. Wealth acquires what it needs to gain and sustain power, and it often does so by financial attrition alone. It simply wears the other side out of money.

The third power that I suggested is the power of knowledge. It is the awareness to know what the right thing is to do at the right time. Its tools are creativity and critical thinking. It is the wisdom to know when to fight or when to survive by flight. Bullies and the wealthy do not have a cornered awareness of the market. For them, their power is just brawn or bucks.

Awareness is the old equalizer to these others. Each of us has the potential for knowledge and wisdom. Brains are handed out to all of us. The question becomes how we develop that brain and how we put it to use.

But awareness is much more comprehensive than just book learning, although book learning is, in my judgment, important. Awareness is about street knowledge—knowing that the bully really is not seeking to borrow fifty dollars from you. Awareness is being wise enough to wear your seat belt or to wear a helmet when you ride your bicycle. It is the wisdom to avoid risk. It is the wisdom to not act impulsively. It is the knowledge not to eat the yellow snow. It is the wisdom to follow your gut instincts.

Awareness also comes from reading, writing, and action. It is the experiences of life. It is the benefit of practice. For example, you may have read all of the books on how to play basketball, you may have dreamed it, and you may have envisioned it; until you play it, practice it, and internalize it, you do not really know very much about basketball. Likewise, until you have articulated the best practices of basketball and have taught basketball's best practices, you do not really know and understand the game. You do not really understand the nature of your game and how to plan your strategy. It is one thing to know it. It is quite another to do it. That is awareness.

Awareness is also the ability to consider things in detached reflection. It is the truths we come to realize after we think we know it (including the realization that we really don't know it) that ultimately count in life that will make a difference. Awareness is the gradual accumulation of additional baseline knowledge and the nuances of that information long after we thought we understood the subject.

We now live in a day and age where information and, maybe, more importantly, misinformation are everywhere. I have likened the challenge to that of each of us trying to find twigs of truth in oceans of "information." That is more imposing than the proverbial "needle in a haystack." It is your responsibility to think critically and seek the truth. Sometimes you have to stop blaming the clown and ask yourself why you continue to participate in the circus. Finally, knowledge of history, of events, and unintended consequences is extremely important. Ignorance of historical events and their consequences may result in greater risk in your own time.

As we discussed in the chapter on action, planning is often more important than implementation. It certainly reduces the perception of uncertainty. The Harvard economist Mikel Harry has spent his whole life studying the costs of production and what the greatest influences on profits are. He has concluded that in the business environment, the actual costs of planning represent 5% of the direct and indirect costs of goods or services provided and sold; yet planning leverages or impacts those costs by 70%. In short, planning, above getting the cheapest and best materials, the cheapest and best labor, and controlling overhead, is the greatest factor in profit. Above all, it helps to think about it first.

Sir Frances Bacon observed that knowledge itself was power. Just having the confidence in yourself, the knowledge, and the belief that you can do it is often enough. If you can dream it, you can do it. This is not to say that you should dwell in the realm of delusional expectations. In my case, it would not be likely, although I may dream it, that I would become Michael Jordan. Size, eye-hand coordination, the ability to jump and shoot, age, and other physical factors preclude that expectation from becoming reality. Jordan was a great basketball player, but he was not so great as a baseball player. But the knowledge and belief, the perception, or the view that you can do it sometimes is enough. On the other hand, if you know you cannot do it, you will not be able to do it. It is usually that simple.

Benjamin Franklin once observed that an investment in knowledge always returns the best interest. I have yet to hear from anyone that knowledge is bad. The issue may be what one believes to be "important" knowledge. For our purposes, what is probably more "important" is that you recognize the power of knowledge itself. Good or bad is subjective. All knowledge is helpful. It fashions your view of life. It fashions how you see things.

Another meaningful source of knowledge is intuition, although some would say that it is an emotion. In my judgment, women do this much better than men, but we all need to tune into our intuition more often than we currently do. Intuition, to me, is our inherent ability to grasp the reality of a situation or circumstance without logic or reasoning. It is a sort of pure reasoning or pure knowing. It is the ability to take a piece of a jigsaw puzzle and know where it goes. The greatest gift of intuition is the feeling that in your "gut," something is not right. And it is recognizing that if something "feels" not right, it is probably wrong. It is the inherent insight to know better. That is awareness in its purest sense.

Intuition is also understanding and knowing that there are some things that are true that cannot be seen. The absence of evidence is not evidence of absence. But intuition comes along mightily if it is coupled with critical thinking. A good, sound dose of skepticism will make you less disposed to foolish conduct.

More about character

It seems to me that in this day and age, it is the gimmick that has come to the forefront as being more important than basic character. There are all kinds of books, tapes, seminars, and symposiums on how to sell, what are the tricks of the trade, and what are the easy ways to get someone to buy something he or she may not really need or even care to have. While such knowledge may be useful to you, in the process, you may be selling yourself short. My judgment is that character is far more important. And certainly, honorable conduct has its own rewards. Coach Wooden has said that a clear conscience is always the softest pillow at the end of the day.

It is your awareness of your own character that in the end is important than the sale at all costs. In the end, it may be more important to walk away than make a bad deal or a dishonorable deal. But you must have the character, the resolve, to say, "No, thank you," even if it may hurt your pocketbook. In the end, it may be that your character is all that is left. That is always enough in my judgment.

There is also the illusion of authority or power. Police, soldiers, and others who are dressed in uniforms, with epaulets on their shoulders, bars on their shirts, badges, medals, weapons, and, of course, a huge wad of keys, are such an illusion. They have handcuffs and flashlights. But do they get their power from character or from the stick? Or is it just an illusion? Uniforms and keys and cuffs and guns do not mean that the power deserves respect. There is an old Hispanic saying that reads:

 El chango en traje' siege seindo chango.

Translated, it means:

A monkey in a silk suit is still a monkey.

Your Personal Power Pyramid

Power and authority only become legitimate when accepted and respected. Without acceptance, authority is but an illusion. It can be rejected, and it is unsustainable in the long term. That does not mean that you do not have to conform in the short run to survive. You do what you must do to survive, to minimize the inconvenience.

External power of a real, lasting sense, however, in my judgment, comes from character. That is authentic power. Long term, it is the most credible, legitimate, and genuine external power that exists. Character endures the "politics" of the "swagger stick." It is not inflicted. It is not coerced. Gandhi figured that out. Such power is the essence of leadership. Human beings of character lead by example. Their conduct, under any circumstances, whether adverse or celebratory, becomes the inspiration for others. Others agree to serve, not based upon dominance or supremacy of position. They are not obligated to do so because they are subjected to do so, but they do so because they believe they can make a difference. That is legitimate power. That is what you should strive for in your life.

Do the right thing

Knowledge provides a sound foundation for character. It permits you to decide to do the right thing, at the right time, in the right place, with the right people, and for the right reasons. Then you will have no regrets. Responsible action mitigates the risks to yourself and others. Always take the time to do the right thing and for the right reasons.

Awareness as other forms of power

Often, legitimate power comes from one's position in an organization and one's ability to lead. There exist, then, tools by which one can exercise that power. It may be that the power is exercised by the carrot (reward) or the stick (coercion). Personal power, on the other hand, may largely come from knowledge. Expertise in a particular field may provide that power.

Awareness also provides the foundation for what is often called reverent power. Leaders often have that source of power, in that through their convictions, their clearness of vision, their confidence in their ability to implement and realize their goals, their perceived power as agents of change, and their achievement of results, these people are honored and respected by their peers. A good example, in my judgment, of a person with referent power is Winston Churchill. That was inspiring leadership. This was a man of deep-seated character.

Awareness often provides one a basis for another kind of personal power—the power of connectivity. Sometimes, it is not what you know, but who you know, that provides the awareness to get it done. Connectivity comes from creating alliances or interrelationships. It may be that connectivity gives one personal power from the informational grapevine, insider knowledge of the true dynamics of a situation, circumstance, or opportunity. The reliability of information permits one to make better decisions faster. So always maintain and nurture your alliances and interrelationships, and put your ear to the ground from time to time.

Personal awareness growth

Awareness only grows if you cultivate it, plant it, water it, weed it, and ultimately harvest it. It does not come about on its own. You must seek information and challenge its validity through critical thinking. You must use your eyes, ears, nose, and fingers to see what is going on. You must use the awareness you have, or you will lose it. If you cannot internalize it and use it, it is worthless knowledge. And finally, you must share that awareness. If it is not shared, it will not grow. Awareness is like love; it will not grow unless nurtured. Awareness comes from asking questions, not from having answers. Always remind yourself that ignorance (lack of awareness) is not always what you don't know, but what you think you know that is just not so. That is where awareness can even things out. That is how you evolve.

There is an old Murphy's law corollary that concludes that all of us should never attribute to malice what can be adequately explained by ignorance. You must always consider the source. Is the conduct or statement based on fact, logic, or emotion? If it is not relevant to you, then it should not carry much importance in the long run. There is an old English maxim:

Never wrestle with a pig. You both get dirty, and
the pig likes it.

There is also the old cowboy logic that you should never approach a bull from the front, a horse from the rear, or a fool from any direction. Do not waste your time engaging or debating with fools.

Keeping up with change

With change now occurring at warp speed, it is extremely important in your awareness quest that you embrace change as the constant. The awareness of change requires you to continually learn and explore. If you do not, then you, too, will become obsolete. A manual typewriter is not worth much these days, and neither will you be worth much unless you continue to learn, explore, think critically, and grow your own awareness of all things that affect you. Knowledge does not have a "sell by" date or an expiration date. It is a continuous process of learning.

You are not a cat

You have heard that curiosity killed the cat. The good news is that you are not a cat. Never stop questioning things, ideas, circumstances, situations, and even what you may believe is fundamental knowledge. Nothing is fundamental about it. Keep an open but curious mind. See learning as fun, not as drudgery. Curiosity makes you a better problem-solver. It will help you overcome your fears about someone or something. It is also likely that curiosity will give you a big daily dose of humility.

Awareness comes from listening

When I was in grade school, one of my teachers observed that we have two ears and one mouth. As a result, we should listen at least twice as much as we talk. You will not learn much while your lips are moving. Moreover, a closed mouth gathers no foot, so to speak. Never miss an opportunity to shut up and listen. You will be surprised by what you will learn.

Perfection to a fault

There is nothing that we can fault about excellence, is there? It is something we all should strive for throughout our lives. Yet if we are compulsive about excellence and we seek perfection, chances are that it will never happen. The expectation of perfection will be a failure. Practice probably won't make you perfect, but it will make you better. So rather than setting your goal at the unattainable, do as our friend Michael Jamison would suggest: Become a precisionist.

A precisionist always sees how close he can come to perfection. He is hoping for the bull's eye but will settle for the very best he can do. Precisionists are also pragmatics. They have practical goals. If close is good enough, then close it is. It is done. Results are more important than perfection.

That having been said, remember that doing poor work or taking less effort than is necessary to do it correctly will get you nowhere—halfway up the stony mountain—mediocrity. Jordan should recall the admonition of his high school teacher, Coach Gray, "If you don't have time to do it right, how do you believe you will have the time to do it over?"

You have seen perfection manifest itself to a fault in your own lives—in sports and in school. There are many excellent athletes, and they seek perfection in their skills. They practice, practice, and practice. But when it comes down to it, in the heat of the game, they fail. They cannot finish it. The same is true in studies. Have you ever seen someone research a paper to the point of diminishing returns and then go beyond? Book smarts are nothing unless you can use that knowledge in a productive way. It is one thing to know it. It is a far different thing to use it or do it. Some of the greatest coaches in football, basketball, or other team sports were not very good, very skilled players. Yet they knew how to teach and to motivate individual players and turn all of those skills into a team that achieved results. That is knowledge in action. Knowledge is potential power. It is action that turns on the switch.

It is also important that you keep the fundamental principle of competition in proper perspective. Competition is not just about winning, although I have heard that winning is everything. It is not. Competition is all about making you better, developing your character. Sometimes the best thing that can happen to you is that you lose. Then you have the motivation to work harder, to excel in your game. Lastly, consider this. When the competition is between you and the game, in the long run, there are no losers, only winners. When you compete against yourself, you can only improve yourself. Life is the game. That is a much more important game than football, basketball, baseball, or whatever. At least, it is in my judgment. Knowing that, alone, is an inherently good thing, and that is the knowledge that will hold you well on course after the team sport is gone.

Alan Greenspan said, "Education is the primary engine for economic growth." This is true in either the macroeconomic or microeconomic sense. I suggest, however, that "education" is not just limited to reading, writing, and arithmetic, although such subjects, I concede, certainly help. Education necessarily includes humanities, liberal arts, and other such subjects. One gains an expanded perspective in abstract thought when exposed to art, music, foreign language, philosophy, psychology, and other such subjects. Your ability to think abstractly will be increasingly important across a broad range of professions. The ability to hypothesize, to interpret, to communicate, and to think logically is greatly enhanced, and such tools will be essential to your ability to think critically and, in my judgment, will be necessary for continued innovation. That is why you must read widely, keep up with current events, and keep "sharpening the saw," as Stephen Covey encourages. Would you rather work with a sharp saw or a dull saw? Systematically, you must stop sawing and sharpen the saw.

Finally, it is necessary in the context of awareness that each of us learns to work and function within our own natural rhythm of existence. That is to say that you must learn and work when your body tells you it is the best time each day. Some of us "eagles" work well in the morning. Some of you, as "owls," work better at night. But we are both wise. There are daily cycles that work best for us—

when we can function at our optimum. In psychology, these are called circadian rhythms. They are biological clocks that are inherent in our own DNA. Learn when you work the best and work then. But remember, there are always those out there with nothing to do who will always want you to do nothing with them—those who are majoring in minor things. Such "Floo-Floo birds" always flock together.

So is it true with the circadian rhythm of the harvest, or, as Covey calls it, the harvest mentality? If you want success, you must plant the seed of success. You must nurture that seed. You must weed it, water it, aerate the soil, and care for your seed. Then it will mature. Next, you must harvest it in a timely manner. That is how you get your crop in. If you believe you can plant the seed tonight and get a pumpkin in the morning, you will fail. If you want to be a successful wrestler (just ask Jordan), you cannot just practice the night before. If you want abundance, you have to work at it. It is not the lottery. Knowing and applying that awareness of life will lead to your success in whatever you start out to do.

More about time

Over the years, I have come to develop an understanding of the importance of time as a commodity. When you sell time and advice as your stock in trade, the realization often comes at your expense. Always be aware of the influence of time in the physical world. Arrive early, and you will have to wait for others. What if the opportunity comes early? Arrive late, and the others may be gone, and the opportunity may be gone. It is necessary to take time to think, in detached reflection, about what is about to happen. Time is also another equalizer to force and money, just as knowledge acts as an equalizer, as well. We all have the same amount of time. It is a limited commodity. Awareness of the influence of time on any project will hold you well in advantage. Remember that other people, natural events such as tornadoes, and other external circumstances can take your possessions from you, but they cannot take time from you. You do that to yourself by not using your time wisely.

Even in prison, your time belongs to you. You decide every day whether you want that time to count or not. You can use it in sleeping, in confrontation, or whatever, or you can use it for your own purposes. Do not waste it. Use it. Lost time can never be regained. It is gone forever. So use your time wisely. Engage when the circumstances favor you. Disengage when confrontation is folly. When planning, always consider the element of time and how it will affect your results. What you think matters; time matters as well. Use it or lose it.

Self-awareness

As we discussed in the chapter on attitude, most of life is an inside job. That is to say that you control your life by the reactions that you decide to make concerning external matters that affect you. Awareness, as a personal power, contains within it a critical element that the Greek philosophers characterized as "know thyself." Self-awareness is the ability to understand yourself. What are your strengths? Are you a good speaker? Do you write well? Do you prefer memos to meetings? Are you a team player or a "do it on your own" person? Do you prefer numbers to words? Do you have spatial or other special abilities? All of us have significant strengths and, unfortunately, material weaknesses. But you must understand yourself. The most important awareness is self-perception in real terms. Know yourself.

This is not a simple process, and it never ends. Sell yourself short, and you do not get what you deserve. Let your ego get in the way, and you will probably get what you deserve. It usually will not be what you wanted. The landscape of personal awareness will change with time, experiences, knowledge, and your capacity to discern what is important to you. For example, if you want money, that is the result. That comes from service. Serve others, and the money will be there. It always works that way. You must give to receive.

As we will discuss later in the chapter on alliances, there is no such person as a "self-made man." What you think of yourself and how you honestly assess your worth to yourself and others, will make a great difference in your success. Never forget, however, that a thousand piranha will always take down the shark. Julius Caesar learned that the hard way about two millennia ago. Always be aware of yourself, and never take yourself too seriously.

Awareness requires you to be open to everything yet attached to nothing. I really do mean nothing. If you covet material things in front of faith in spirit, that all will end someday. You will not get out of this world alive, and you will take nothing with you. You must embrace change as the constant. There is a story told of the great Italian artist Michelangelo, who, when asked, at the age of eighty-seven, what he did each day, replied, "Ancora imparo." "I am still learning." I hope I'm at around eighty-seven and can report the same.

Pappy Barr used to say, "Too soon, we get old; too late, we get smart!" Wisdom sometimes never comes to us, so when it does, we should not reject it out of hand because it comes late. So keep learning and continue to evolve. You will make yourself and the world a better place to exist.

Your third cornerstone is awareness.

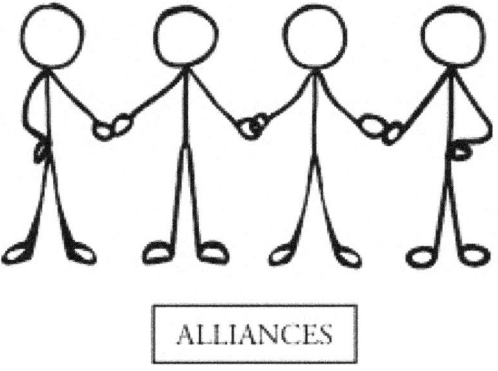

ALLIANCES

All thought draws life from contacts and exchanges.
—Fernand Bandel

Chapter 5
Your Fourth Power: Alliances

While it is important that you make every day count, there is a practical limitation on what you individually can achieve great things. That is time. We cannot and should not "work" all of the time. We must take time to eat, sleep, and even play. We need to take time to exercise, remain aware of advances in technology and society, and all of those diversions, in theory, take away from our efficient efforts at the improvement of ourselves and those around us. It is Stephen Covey's sharpening of the saw. If you do not stop and sharpen the saw, if you are just sawing, pretty soon, the results will be poor. Remember that efforts do not equate to achievement. So you, individually, are limited by the time that you can commit to the purposes that are important to you.

How can we leverage that time, then, and get more out of it? One way we can do so is by developing alliances with others. Interrelationships with others, who can assist us in our tasks or others who provide other attributes, coupled with our attributes, will make all of us stronger, wiser, and more productive.

Edwin Carpenter

There is an old story about two Englishmen who were stranded on an island. The British are known for their love of gardens. Each man set out to build his own garden for food and for flowers. Soon, both had cultivated their gardens, planted their seeds or plants, and were then weeding, watering, and nurturing their own gardens. One evening, as they were both talking about their gardens and how to make them better, they both decided that they would establish an island garden club. They would then pool their resources and extra time for the club garden. The next thing anyone knew was that there was then a third garden with both men working together.

Such is the nature of alliances. It is the principle of one plus one equals three. By working together, each man provided his wisdom, strength, and other personal resources to make a third collective garden for the benefit of both. Ultimately, these men figured out that they could collectively have one garden, bigger and better than the three they had cultivated on their own.

In economics, this outcome is called the principle of absolute advantage. Each of us has skills. With two people dividing the job into skills that are best suited for them, and they combine their skills, then more gets done in less time. Each person realizes the advantage of doing what he or she does best. Each person works together and in unison, rather than in isolation. It may be, then, that one plus one equals eleven with more free time to spare. That is the compounding power of alliances.

Your Personal Power Pyramid

As we look at history, it seems that the bad guys, the bullies, of the world figured it out first. It is always easier for ten to take down one. It is always easier for ten to take from one. And it is easier to steal than it is to cultivate (in theory). So it could be that humankind then had to join to protect itself from the common enemy, humankind. There is also strong evidence out there that early humanoids had to band together, create alliances, and develop social skills as the best method of no longer being the prey of predators such as lions or tigers. There was a congregate power in the herd. Yet I suspect that it was also as simple as one human sharing excess food, one human watering and weeding his neighbor's garden while the neighbor was hunting, or other similar acts of social bonding. Evolution of humankind has had such great success (some would argue also great failures) through the joining of human resources. Therefore, I would suggest that social friendship is nurtured by human nature.

We also know that while survival may be a zero-sum game in some contexts (you die and I live), there are other examples, possibly more pervasive and certainly less pernicious, where humankind advances its existence. One such example is the principle of reciprocal altruism. That is to say that we do good things for others out of the goodness of our hearts. We do not expect anything in return; yet there is an unwritten law of nature that we should all help each other. It is almost intuitive. By helping my neighbor, when I need something, he will be there to help me or to help someone else. It becomes reciprocal, not because I expect something in return, but because that is how we intuitively know that we are advancing human existence and our collective causes.

We also know that a sense of interdependence with others leads to much greater results. It is the evolution even of each of us. When we are born, we are dependent. We rely upon our mothers and fathers to care for us. Then we move to a stage of independence where we do not want help from anyone (adolescence) and where we are resistant to the wisdom of others. Ultimately, if we evolve individually to an appropriate stage of maturity, we become interdependent. We associate with others, we rely upon others, and we are all the better for it. Rather than "zero-summers" (I win; you lose), it is then a "win-win" result. That is the very nature of interdependence—of alliances.

If you put humankind's achievements in perspective, as we discussed earlier, there is nothing without motion. Energy utilization is how we get progress; how we survive. If we do nothing, we get nothing in return. The question, then, is how humankind advances (even recognizing its enormous capacity for evil)? I suggest that the advancement of humankind is the result of thousands or maybe even millions of years of expanded energy for the collective good of all. One might even be able to sort of measure the advancement of humankind in terms of the amount of effort harnessed individually and collectively annually, when humans have harnessed greater individual and collective energy to make their lives and the lives of others better. Basically, as we all work together, we all evolve into something greater than one—sort of a ladder of good deeds, of good energy utilized, for the betterment of all.

That is not to say, however, that all alliances are good. Some are not so good for you. It is said that birds of a feather… The three of you all joke at me (because you are young and "bulletproof" or at least believe yourselves to be) that I prefer to get up in the morning and get moving. On the other hand, to extend the avian metaphor, I see you three as hooting with the owls in the night. I prefer to fly with the eagles in the morning. The point is that you become, oftentimes, what are the traits and characteristics of those you flock with. So be careful what group ideals and goals are important to you, and join the group because those ideals and goals are important to you. You will be judged by others based on who and when you associate with fellow humans. If the alliance has unimportant goals, so will you, and so will you be viewed.

Moreover, associations can be negative and can have negative consequences. There is a tendency when larger groups get together that not everyone pulls his or her own weight. Most will only pull what they believe is needed. Pick your associates using a fundamental principle I have used since my own personal history and experience of picking poor partners in the business of "lawyering." That principle is this: Choose your associates by asking the simple question, "Would I want to go to war with this person beside me?" If the answer in your gut is, "No!" then don't have the expectation of a long-term, mutually beneficial association. If you are not all pulling together, then there can be little or no progress, as the internal resistance will make the enterprise less than successful. There will be better ways to expend your energy and use your resources.

The history books are full of accounts of evil associations, from Genghis Khan to Adolph Hitler. This necessarily brings us to what Patton called the highest form of human endeavor—war.

As Patton put it, compared to war, all other forms of human endeavor shrink to insignificance. Why war? What is it good for? Why are such associations necessary? It may be that such associations are not necessary, but they are reality.

The fact is that there are many humans out there with evil purposes in mind. Such humans as Hitler and his ilk seek power for their own sake. Yet we know that the Khans and the Hitlers come and go. Notwithstanding these setbacks in the advancement of humankind, those evil ones always fail. Mostly, they do themselves in. Evil always runs its course.

I suggest that the "barbarians" at the gates often serve a purpose. They often are the competition necessary for humankind to advance. They are part of the evolution of society. As a society grows stagnant, it is often necessary that the society be "destroyed." It is Joseph Schumpeter's "creative destruction" at work.

Organizations over time will become so stagnant, so layered, that nothing gets done. The hierarchy is frozen and dysfunctional.

Incompetency, waste, redundancy, and nonproductivity reign. It is sort of the entropy of cultural advancement. In such circumstances, the old structure must be torn apart and put back together for it to continue to evolve, to continue to adapt, and to continue to advance. Entropy is extinction in its broadest sense.

For example, the Germanic tribes were the downfall of the Roman Empire. Yet we know that in the end, the Roman Empire was inherently evil and corrupt. It largely evolved on the backs of slaves. So who were the barbarians? Were the Germanic tribes the "bad guys" or the Romans themselves? (This is not to say that there were no positive contributions of the Roman Empire to the advancement of civilization. There were many and many good and innocent people who perished when the corrupt system fell.)

We must continue to work with our alliance partners to make it mutually beneficial. When we fail to do so, the alliance will fail. When we are so engrossed in ourselves that we fail to recognize the good in others, then we are bound to fail. That is the nature of evolution; inbreeding leads to destruction.

The same may be said of the size of an alliance. Alliances are much like chains. They are only as good as the weakest link. Moreover, we do not always add to an alliance by adding links to the chain. They must have some purpose. Otherwise, they are just extra weight. Likewise, alliances are not elastic. They do not stretch well. Alliances that you choose should be chosen with wisdom, not whimsy, and should be valuable and hard to forge. Otherwise, they will be weak and worthless to you.

To foster personal power, however, you must believe in and envision a productive community—a community of sustained production. One good thing done to another produces another good thing. You have to trust in others (within the realm of reality). The advancement of the goals of others—to serve—is the advancement of your own goals. Each of our actions in the service of others has the potential to create new outcomes—reciprocal altruism at its best. That is how humankind has evolved.

Part of the process of alliance seeking, however, is the necessity of asking ourselves, "Is this the right thing to do? What collective results do I want to achieve—do I consider to be important?" You must be honest, genuine, and authentic with yourself. You must constantly revisit your fundamental beliefs, your source of character, and you must continuously realign your alliances based upon your view of things today. You must ultimately be accountable to yourself. What can you contribute, and what do you get back in return? How can I serve?

Finally, remember that humans only give value to the alliance to the extent that they contribute to the good of the order. If loyalty is conditional, then everything becomes situational, and the alliance will fail. As we should know, evolution is not linear. It has cycles of convergent activities, and it will have cycles of divergent activity.

Mistakes are inevitable. All other things being equal, the person or group that makes fewer strategic errors is successful. Mistakes are lessons learned (or earned), but you must not dwell on them. There is no absolute security in life. Yet there is opportunity if you look for it, even in adversity. Be mindful that if you are not progressing, then inherently, you are regressing because the rest of the world is moving on past you.

For any alliance to work, each member of the alliance must trust the other to do what needs to be done. However, trust without accountability is not a wise route to consider or take. Even with equal partners, you will have to be vigilant. You have to measure and monitor the partner's commitment and industriousness to get the job done, to get results. Remember this simple rule: You can always trust someone if you do not have to. Check and recheck. "Inspect what you expect," as Pappy Barr would say. Then the alliance will truly work.

Self-made man

You have surely heard of men and women being characterized as self-made. This is not possible, in my judgment. We are all shaped and molded by our environment and, frankly, our own DNA. Whether it is nature or nurture, the fact is that other people and other circumstances influence and develop our personal character. As you look back on your life, you will reflect upon teachers, coaches, a parent or grandparent, team members, and fraternity brothers who may have helped you in your Waterloo journey. You may also discover that there were negative influences that you had to overcome to be successful. You have not gotten here on your own. Whether you have lived in the city or the country will influence your life, as well.

That is why alliances are so important. You cannot do it as well on your own. By creating sound and solid alliances, each of us brings our unique talents and experiences to the group. You will discover in the process that this sharing of oneself is very much like an echo. What you give, you get back, often in multiples, amplified to a higher level of awareness.

Priority setting among allies

There is one huge caveat in this whole business of alliances. Properly functioning, the alliance will permit better division of labor, the one-plus-one-equals-three results we discussed earlier. However, it is important to the alliance that you do what you do best. It is important that you do first things first. There will be "allies" who don't do or can't do what they were assigned to do. There will be "allies" who suffer from indecision, worry, procrastination, and a score of other human frailties. But if you succumb to their urgent needs, you will not do what is necessary to make the alliance successful. Simply put, stick to your own priorities, not the pressures of the demands or concerns of others. You have to decide what is important to the success of the alliance. You have to decide what is truly urgent. To the extent that your focus is diverted to the important and urgent matters of others, you will not get done what you need to get done. Plan and set your priorities, and do those things first. Then you will have done your part. You will be someone to count upon; you will have accountability. You will all achieve the leverage of the power of alliances.

Alliances with spirit and spouse

As you will see in the next chapter on affirmation, I have suggested that one great alliance to make is with spirit. If you and your spirit have a central focus, if you are centered with spirit, all will be well. That "alliance" is further developed next.

After your alliance with spirit, I would encourage you to develop a personal relationship with a woman like your mother or your grandmother, "Muz." While there are challenges with such long-term relationships, such alliances will cover your personal weaknesses and make them largely unimportant in your ability to broaden your personal power base. The economic principle of absolute advantage is demonstrated well in such marriage alliances. There are great, wise, intuitive, loving women out there, and they make wonderful partners in life. But ask the question, Do I want to go to war with this person beside me? Then you will know.

Movements toward greatness or excellence always require serious and committed collective effort. The opposite of that is the movement toward decline, which only requires complacency. Nature's world in its ultimate state is entropy. And while the future cannot be predicted, it can be nurtured, persuaded, and managed if we are wise enough to move forward in a measured, collective effort. The future cannot be ruled in my judgment. But the future is as malleable as your ingenuity to do something about it now.

Your fourth cornerstone is alliances.

Faith consists in believing when it is beyond the power of reason to believe.

—Voltaire

Chapter 6
Your Fifth Power: Affirmation

Whether we like it or not, embedded in our DNA, or otherwise, is a simple realization that Homo sapiens are spiritual creatures. For all you scientists out there, I understand and appreciate that we should not expect there to be a spirit gene. Yet intuitively, we know (or should know) that there is something more than the physical. I suggest to you that the greatest source of your personal power comes from a sacred commitment to spirit. In my judgment, one cannot fully realize or actualize individual or collective power unless one commits to and understands that all power comes from a spiritual base. Without that knowledge, all your worldly wisdom coming from knowing, understanding, and internalizing action, attitude, awareness, and alliances will get you nowhere in the long run. You may achieve proprietary success, but at some point in your life, you will have to face the ultimate and absolute truth—your body and its biological thought processes will come to an end. This is not to suggest, however, that materiality is not of your venue on earth. I choose to define "material" as important, not just who dies with the most toys. That is not material in the long run. It is not important in the long run.

I do not have the ability to define the source of this spiritual power for you. I do not believe that human beings can fully define in human terms such a concept. Left to our meager and inadequate resources, we always try to define the source of spirit in our own terms, with our own limitations. I submit that about the time you think you have got it right, then I am almost certain that you do not. St. Augustine said it better than I can, "Si comprehendis non est Deus." (If you think you comprehend it, it is not God.) That is not the "creator"; it is something that you have created. My view is that the source of spirit requires no substantiation of what is created, or that it was created, or, for that matter, that it is or is not the "creator." In my opinion, defining spirit in human terms only demonstrates our mediocrity—halfway up the mountain.

Nevertheless, over the years, I have learned that if I solely rely upon myself and solely believe in myself, then I become more important to myself than the source of spirit, and then I covet myself and all things material—sort of a "mine, mine, mine" mentality. When we do so, we have lost the spirituality of ourselves, and we have traded down to our own passions of the flesh. I suggest only that such trades have adverse consequences. The question becomes, in the hierarchy of power, what do you place first? The apex of your personal power pyramid is the affirmation of your own spirituality. If you are arrogant, then you place your hope in the property. And whether you believe it or not, it is what you will become. It is where your heart will be. You have committed yourself to what is created by you or by others. You will have substituted that property commitment for the spiritual commitment that is the essence of humankind. You will be the victim of pride. I suggest that admiration of your own reflection (or your own accomplishments) in the mirror is not likely to lead you to further "success" than the internal introspection or reflection upon your true purpose.

While my small mind cannot define the source of spirit for you, I can tell you this. When you decide to commit to spirit, all kinds of wonderful and positive things will happen. When a human being acts, the spirit acts. When a human being does nothing, the spirit does nothing. One must change that potential energy into kinetic energy. If you decide to design and build a house, the spirit will provide you with those plans. The spirit will provide you with the materials, the workmen, and the place to build that house. If you build a ship, the spirit will provide you with the sea to sail it upon and the ports of call. When you act, the spirit always gives something back to you; it is the source of abundance.

On the other hand, if you take no action, if you give nothing, you will get nothing in return. The source always works that way. You cannot give away what you do not possess. You get back from the spirit what you gave up. If you believe the resources are limited and do not give away, you will get back what you expected to receive—exactly nothing.

Your Personal Power Pyramid

In my judgment, human beings are born with that inherent knowledge. It is intuitive to us. Yet over our development into "adulthood" (whatever that means), most of us lose sight of our spirituality. We sort of send ourselves out into exile. In a sense, we permit our spirit to be diminished so that we can learn to live in the everyday mundane world. But once you affirm and reaffirm your spiritual nature, then the self-imposed exile is at an end. The reaffirmation must never end. You must return from exile in your own way, in your own time, and on your own terms. The sooner you do so, the better, in my opinion.

The universe is what it is. It will expand, stars will come and go, planets will come and go, there will be black holes, and there is and will continue to be bright and dark matter. None of that I can control, nor do I suggest that you can control it either. For what it is worth, my judgment is that when one believes that one is the center of the universe, that belief is bound for failure. I humbly suggest that it is a tough business to keep all of the stars and planets spinning the way they need to spin, keep the comets and asteroids cruising through space as they should, and keep these galaxies separated.

Mistakes might be catastrophic to both your existence and a significant part of the universe. It is a daunting task to carry "your universe" on your shoulders and to constantly manipulate your universe to work for your purposes. On the other hand, if you let go and control what you can, life will be a lot easier. You might even have time for rest and relaxation. The universe may not be divinely ordered, but it is ordered. It is a tall order to suggest that you alone can change it. And if you can't change it, you have to change the way you look at it.

This brings me necessarily to the business of religion. Certainly, I do not need to kill additional trees by touting a religion of choice. Moreover, I should not be so arrogant (self-centered) to presume that my god is the only god and the correct god and that all others are in error. Fixed and rigid religious beliefs are, in my humble judgment, largely an infantile disease, sort of like the "chicken pox" of humankind, as Einstein suggested. Experience and history demonstrate to me that many zealously religious humans, crusading along and practicing their single dogma, are often exceedingly evil human beings.

Here is but one terrible example. In 1562, the Catholic Bishop Diego de Landa ordered all the Mayan codices, chronically 800 years of Mayan history and knowledge, piled up and burned, and, "in the name of faith," executed all of the Mayan priests, astronomers, and mathematicians.

In short, I urge you to have faith, but not faith without critical thought, without skepticism. That is just pure superstition. All things evil often begin with a "noble" cause. It is when you think you know it all that the good is transformed into evil.

All religious doctrines and their institutions predate the development of modern science and the scientific method. Many scientists give us strong evidence that all scripture has been made by humankind, not by the creator. Why is it that humans seek to define the source of spirit on their own terms? I struggle with the religious notions that spirit is jealous, seeks retribution, is a loving spirit, is intelligent, is angry, bargains with us to get us to act honorably, is vengeful, or has any other human characteristics whatsoever.

The concept of sin (a problem) that is corrected by salvation (solution) is very much like the old protection gambit. Or how about the whole premise of the "bargain principle," as I call it, in certain religious doctrines that I am greatly troubled by in my own journey back? That principle basically goes like this: If you accept our "God" as your savior, then our "God" will no longer dislike you and will allow you to go to heaven; or there is the obvious corollary—if you do not accept our "God" as your savior, then our "God" will banish you to hell. I suggest that the true spirit is not domineering. Spirit is not intolerant. This is the whole "carrot" and "stick" program of parent and child, employer and employee, teacher and student, and so forth. Why? Why should this be so? This is the guilt trip before you even commit the crime. You begin existence in a plea bargain with "God." What sort of "creator" is this? A creator who makes junk in "his" own image and then criticizes the result. Why couldn't the source be impersonal? There probably is no "ego" in true spirit.

There is a great deal of evil and misery in life. Part of your commitment to the spirit ought to be recognition of events that are often monstrous and terrible in life. You must accept that for what it is, and while there may be periods of less evil and less misery, the pendulum will always swing back. So it can be said with respect to all societies. They may be, in the end, ultimately evil, sorrowful, unfair, and dangerous to the self-interest of individual survival. Evil always runs its course, though. The trick, in my judgment, is to learn to pass through life humbly and to teach fellow human beings how to learn to live with life, as well. Martin Luther King said it this way:

We must accept finite disappointment, but never lose infinite hope.

The aim of your commitment to spirituality is the wisdom and power to serve others, make a difference in your own humble way. To serve—not to rule—should be your mission. That is how you return from exile. Max Ehrmann may have said it best in his statement on life, "Desiderata," when he suggested:

> …You are a child of the universe no less than the trees and the stars; you have a right to be here. And whether or not it is clear to you, no doubt the universe is unfolding as it should. Therefore, be at peace with God, whatever you conceive Him to be. And whatever your labors and aspirations, in the noisy confusion of life, keep peace in your soul. With all its sham, drudgery, and broken dreams, it is still a beautiful world. Be cheerful. Strive to be happy.

Be mindful, however, that if you believe that someone or something is somehow depriving you of your own happiness, that someone is likely you. Attitude is everything. If you are miserable, are suffering, or believe that you would be miserable or be suffering in the future, guess what? You have predestined that you will be.

"Goodness" itself, however, is relative. It is a matter of perspective. It is a matter of emotion. So I submit that being "good," whatever that may mean, will not get the job done. You must have a personal relationship with the spirit.

There is also nothing "noble" about acting or believing that you are superior to others. True "nobility" lies in being superior every day to your former self.

I have also struggled with this whole religious debate and the business of intelligent design. That is to say that the universe was created with a human purpose: anthropic design, if you will. Why? Possibly the design was to create smart, wise dinosaurs, and Homo sapiens is just an unintended consequence. My judgment is that at the rate and direction humankind is progressing, we will not last one-tenth of the time that dinosaurs controlled this earth. We have already pushed and pulled our way through several branches of humanoids, and we continue to destroy the ecosystem of the Earth at a staggering rate. We seem to be marching to self-destruction at an alarming pace, and no meteor or comet impact or volcano eruption will be our demise.

You see, this whole exercise over intelligent design is a physical discussion. Spirit does not design. It does need to be created. It does not need to evolve. Only the housing does. And if the housing does not evolve, extinction is around the corner. Spirit will be there regardless of the form it may take.

So what is wrong with believing that the housing evolved and it took billions of years to do so? Is that more disingenuous than a literalist view that humans were created by God some 6000 years ago? Certainly, modern science suggests that humanlike creatures may have existed on Earth for six million years or so. In Ethiopia, in April of 2006, anthropologists reported that they discovered humanlike fossils that are 4.2 million years old, which filled in a further gap in the chain of evolution. Similarly, anthropologists reported in the same month that some 9,000 years ago, primitive humans were performing dentistry on others.

The emergence of life on Earth, let alone the emergence of humankind, remains one of the greatest and comprehensive mysteries of science. Life may simply be a matter of the emergence of simple chemistry to complex chemistry. This is but another example of the principle of association—alliances through chemical association. In short, scientific inquiry would suggest that metabolism came first, before cells, before replication of molecules, before reproduction of cells, and before life. (This sort of gives us a new perspective on the theory of better living through better chemistry.)

While scientists continue to fill in the gaps, there is still much to be learned. For example, scientists have found a link between a 375-million-year-old fossil called "Tiktaalik" (a fishlike creature with gills, scales, and a primitive wrist and fingerlike bones in its fins), which they believe is the precursor to four-legged amphibians that show up some twenty million years later. Genome mapper Francis Collins has reported that the human genome contains certain nonfunctional fields in the same location as they can be identified on the chromosomes of lower species. That then ends the argument of "God" creating humans separately, not through evolution. Reason would suggest, at least, that "God" would not insert a false gene. The only reason for such a conclusion is that "God" was attempting to mislead us and challenge our faith. Why?

This is serious stuff. We should not ignore how evolution may affect our health and even our survival as a species. It remains to be seen how well Homo sapiens holds up under acute changes in our ecosystem. It may be that humankind will not hold up so well in an environment where it is very hot, where there are holes in the ozone layer, and where carbon dioxide levels are substantially higher than we have ever known. Extinction is the paradigm of this world. Why is there any reason to believe that Homo sapiens will be the exception merely because they believe in a particular god?

As I suggested earlier, religious doctrines and their institutions predate the development of modern science. They have now "found the bones" (as Joseph Campbell would suggest) that invalidate sacred writings as to the beginning. But those "bones" are physical evidence. They are not spiritual evidence. That is why, when you place your faith in physical matters, if you define your spirit in physical terms with personal characteristics, the religious absurdities will always catch up with you.

Finally, a commitment to spirit does not require you to believe that there is a god who has a purpose. The word purpose may have no meaning to the source of spirit. Purpose is, pure and simple, a human notion. For what it is worth, sacred scriptures may give you a human perspective on how to get to heaven, but they have little relevance to the matters of how the heavens go around and what their purpose or purposes may be. They are different matters, entirely. That notwithstanding, your life without purpose that you intend is without direction or cause. If you don't know where you are going, when you get there, you will probably be somewhere else.

Science does not have the last word, either. We continue as human beings to learn more about the infinite nature of the universe. We also continue as human beings to learn more about the infinite nature of subatomic particles. The relative size or smallness of the physical world would even suggest that the universe is made of nothing. Something from nothing! How is that possible? Then there is this business of dark matter and "black holes" that may make up most of the universe. We are just scratching the surface of the universe on these issues. At the end of the universe, so to speak, the universe may be just one black hole, finite, and with a nonzero temperature. Entropy at its final stage. (But then, that may take a long, long time, as there is evidence now that "black-body radiation" may be released or "evaporating" from black holes, reducing the mass and energy of such black holes. So black holes may shrink and vanish in that way, with the black mass and energy associated with that, free-roaming again—a nonentropic event. This phenomenon is known as "Hawking radiation.")

No matter how much we learn, whatever seems to be left to discover and understand remains as complex as what started the inquiry into the cosmos and in the cell in the first place. It may ultimately be that science is a way for us to express our own ignorance of our own collective ignorance. That is healthy self-evaluation in my judgment. That cannot be bad. The secret of the source of the universe and all its components, in my judgment, will never be fully understood by human beings. We are not capable of understanding the infinite. Period.

Religious traditions and writings are deeply embedded in our culture. They are part of our history. They are part of our language, our values, our norms, and our mores. They provide a foundation for the structure of society. They are sacred writings, and it is important to read, understand, and appreciate them. Like scientific expression, they are Homo sapiens' best effort at trying to explain spiritual existence, albeit in human terms. We should value and appreciate ancient writings for what they are. They provide humankind's best efforts at providing the wisdom and strategies to survive in this world of misery. If for no other reason than that, they deserve our respect. That having been said, there is often a paradox in "religious" knowledge. That very knowledge cannot be separated from the circumstances under which it has been acquired.

Sacred scripture has also historically been used for inhuman purposes. Much evil has been leveled upon humankind in the name of a particular god. The claims of the universal validity of a particular god are attempts to elevate that group to a special place in the pecking order of humankind. This is no different than theories of racial or national superiority, also infantile propositions. All religious works are the works of humans, interpreted and often distorted by humans over time. As "man-made" institutions, they are inherently flawed. Like many other things created, it matters greatly how we use those sacred scriptures. Conversely, much "good" has been leveled upon humankind by humble beliefs in a knowing and loving God.

There is a sort of monstrous arrogance in religious truth that you should remain skeptical toward. The fact that one billion people believe something is true does not make it true. Do not accept as true the collective wisdom of individual ignorance. Likewise, a belief is not true merely because it is useful. Those are only compounded zeros. Any god in religion that has been created with personal characteristics is just that. Such a god would appear to be divided against itself. I suggest that human beings created God in their own image, not the opposite. Spirit may take on no form. It may be infinitely great and infinitely small. It likely has no timeline for intervention into the physical world.

Your Personal Power Pyramid

The problem with religion is that it is very much like government. Religious law or doctrines intrude upon an individual's relationship with his or her spirit just as social law intrudes upon an individual's basic social and property rights. There is a sort of paradox here. The goal of religion is to make it easier to create and maintain a relationship with the spirit, but it often does more to damage the relationship than not. Religion, as with all institutions of humankind, over time, ultimately invades personal rights, property rights, and even one's very existence, promotes collusion for the "common good," creates philosophic and proprietary monopolies, and becomes so powerful that no one is safe. It is also a killer. So be careful of your religious alliances and be certain what your real motives are in these associations. The true test may be to ask yourself this question. Are your actions defining your values, or are your values defining your actions?

While religious doctrines may be feeble or noble attempts to find meaning and value in life, despite the suffering nature of life, religious doctrines have always been practical in their approach to the survival of humankind. If the religious theory ceases to be effective in controlling, then it will change; it will evolve. Man made religion, and man can change it. History reports that man often does. You see, in the beginning, man created God. It is impossible, in my judgment, to meet God in any anthropomorphic sense. Moreover, I still have trouble with and do not follow the logic of an omniscient and omnipotent god who has created human beings in his own image, with all of their human frailties, and then blames those same human beings for his own errors in the design and construction, and therefore intervenes and punishes them for it. I see that logic being pure of human concoction. Only humankind could come up with such foolishness. That having been said, if one takes sacred scripture for what it may be intended to be, a conduit to the recognition of spirit and having faith in spirit, then it will assist in the nurturing of that relationship.

I only suggest that the spirit is timeless, infinite, and beyond the comprehension of humankind. Spirit has no concern of the minutia of physical life. It has not revealed itself to humankind in human form. Humans did that to themselves, and they continue to do so. I encourage you, instead, to create a sense of spiritual connection now. Do not wait for him to come down from on high. Spirit does not intervene. It goes with the flow, and spirit is available now. Just hook up. It is mind over matter.

So where does this take us? Einstein once observed that a spirit is manifest in the laws of the universe—a spirit vastly superior to that of man and one in the face of which we, with our modest powers, must feel humble. We have come full circle. The soul of the universe cannot be seen. It cannot be heard. It is inside you and me. It is a matter of trust. It is a matter of faith in a knowing and loving spirit.

In the end, God will be a personal matter—each of us to his own. The business of you and your spirit. Have the courage to accept that the physical world was born from chaos and is ruled by chaos.

Recognize that you cannot "contract" your way out of worldly matters by solitude or by separation. Worldly matters (and maybe time itself) are the daily dance of spirit through you. You are in the universal "dance." Learn to live with life. Embrace it. Rise above it. Then you will have the capacity to survive it. Keep your mind open to the infinite possibilities of the universe. Do not be closed or limited by your beliefs. Have the grace to live in the world, but not to be of the world.

What is truly compelling is that spirit comes to the forefront when all in the physical world has gone bad. That, it seems, is when we need to rely upon the spirit the most. It is how we get through the tough times. It is how we figure out that tough times have a timeline. Tough times do not last. Tough times always pass. Spirit-minded humans do last, however.

Have faith in the source of spirit, and the source will provide for you. That is why you always hear from me to keep the faith. Remember that you must die a little to truly learn to live. With pain and suffering comes the knowledge and wisdom to survive.

This is not to say that if a particular religious structure is important to you, you should not participate with that group or should not associate with those beliefs. That would defy the principle of association, of alliances. As you know, Ginger and I share the beliefs of our friends at the Unity Church in Topeka. We are a small group, but we are mighty in our beliefs about spirit. In addition, I have shared time weekly with a bible study group chaired by my long-time friend, Phil Wolfe. Those in the study group share the journey of understanding, and we often disagree about how one may return from exile. The debate is healthy, however, and we all seek an understanding from each other. These are important relationships to me as I consider the affirmation of spirit. I also gain knowledge (awareness) from such associations. If nothing else, we can learn what we do not have faith in and what we should not affirm. There is wisdom in knowing what to avoid. Lastly, in the context of alliances, what better alliance can there be than to associate with and affirm the power of the spirit? I do not think there can be a better partner to share the journey of life with than the source itself.

Much power and legitimacy in your life can come from such shared beliefs. Just be certain what your motives are. Are they self-centered or source-centered? Unfortunately, my experience tells me that most human beings get only enough of religion to make them miserable with it. While not the fault of spirit, but a limitation on human capacity, nonetheless, many share in this congregate misery. The true wisdom of affirmation comes away from the crowd, between you and the source. That is where it began, and that is where it will end.

Without a commitment to spirit, however, there can be no higher calling than you. The physical world becomes what is important. In the end, even Solomon, the wisest and richest man in recorded history, knew that hope and faith in the context of the physical world are fleeting. The greatest mystery of life is only solved by dying. No human being has ever taken any of the physical aspects of the world into the realm of the spiritual world.

Spirit is infinite. It is timeless. It is the source of all abundance. Make a commitment to your spirit and follow the other principles of your personal power pyramid. All will flow to the top, and you will be the emissary of your spirit on this earth. That is a great and powerful thing, indeed, and humankind will be the better for it.

Here is the way to look at it. What should control? Is it "ego," or is it "spirit"? Is your "ego" on a spiritual experience or journey, or is it really the reverse? Is our spirit having a human experience? I suggest that the latter is more likely true and should be affirmed and reaffirmed daily.

The capstone of your personal power pyramid is the affirmation of your spirit source. You will recall that in the Star Wars sagas, the Force that Obi-Wan Kenobi and Yoda knew, understood, and drew upon is the archetype of the spirit within you. Yoda did not use the Force as the physical power of the playground bully. He was activating that spiritual DNA and turning potential energy into kinetic energy, that energy that is released when you and your spirit will do something to be done. It is mind over matter.

Faith is the source of courage. It is the assurance of things that cannot be explained in physical terms. It is the commitment to things unseen. Here are a couple of stories about the affirmation of the spirit that may restore your faith:

President Eisenhower went to the Massachusetts Institute of Technology to inspect the great computer back in the 1950s. There was this huge room full of computers. The technicians there suggested that the computer could answer any mathematical question, any historical question, and any scientific question for which there was an answer known to man. They suggested that Eisenhower pose a question about the great computer. So Eisenhower did. His question was:

Is there a god?

The great MIT computer churned away at the problem for a while; its data disks spun and spun. After a while, the printer at the console started. The answer was very short. What do you suppose it was? The computer's answer given to President Eisenhower was,

There is one now!

That is the assurance of things unknown. It is also something created by humankind. Now, how about a commitment to things unseen:

> There was a little girl in bible study class that was drawing a picture with crayons. The pastor, upon seeing her work, asked her what she was drawing. The little girl responded that she was drawing a picture of God. The pastor laughed at her and said, "But how can you do that? No one knows what God looks like." The young lady, without a hint of

disappointment, announced, "Well, they will when
I'm finished!"

My friend, Michael Jamison, often ministers us on the
unnecessary struggle between ego and spirit. If we learn to go with
the spirit, the ego will take the ride with the spirit. While Michael
has not said this, his teachings remind me of the observation made
by someone much wiser than me, whose name I cannot recall and
cannot find in my years of notes on life. This wise person suggested
that the word ego is an acronym, and it stands for "edging God out."
We have also joked, although I think it is a correct observation, that
egos are expensive things to own. The maintenance is extraordinarily
expensive, and egos often get in the way of critical thinking. Ego is
in the physical world, as well. If you let go and let the spirit take
over, then there is divine order. You are where you are supposed to
be on the journey.

I have intentionally avoided the issue of whose God to believe
in. You must be left to your own investigation to make those
choices, to decide how you return from exile to your spiritual self.
Knowledge helps because knowledge will give you a greater
perspective, a broader view of the subject. As Frank Sinatra would
say, "I did it my way." We, each of us, have to do it in our own way,
in our own time, in our own place, and on our own terms. And
remember that the journey is spiritual. It never ends. It is not a
destination. It is the routes we take.

Call it what you may, whether it be prayer or meditation, I would also recommend to you that you create for yourself a special, quiet place where you can go to be with your spirit and spend time there reaffirming the importance of the infinite nature of the spirit. Where and how much time you commit is up to you, but I can report to you that such quiet time revitalizes your body and your spirit. You will live longer in this physical world, even with its often-monstrous nature. Find a quiet place and learn to be one with your spirit. Try it. You will soon feel and see the flow of power in affirmation.

Who knows what tomorrow may bring—dancing or death? The cynics of the earth would tell you that life is a sexually transmitted condition that is always fatal. Pessimists say it another way—you will never get out of life alive. But they are in the physical world. Your spirit will get out of life just fine.

All of this having been said, a perspective is that spirit, if ever encountered by humankind in a physical sense, will be more grand and less understandable than any "god" that humankind can conjure up or that any particular religion can ever propose. When we define "God" in human terms, we will always sell spirit short. I believe we lack the intellectual capacity to do so.

It is the faith in knowing that that gives you a higher calling, a higher personal purpose. As was referenced at the beginning of this journey, the gods choose our battles for us. But our purpose is to advance the standard forward as far as we can physically do so—to recognize and realize upon the truth of the duties before us. The proper concern of each of us is the duty to take action. The congregate or ultimate results or consequences should be of little concern, so long as your motives are true of spirit. You must have faith that the end is secured. Let your spirit take control of the how. Usually, the spirit takes care of itself anyway if you have a mentality of abundance. Your duty is to serve humankind. That is where faith comes in. That is how humankind evolves spiritually. That is how you get through life.

In conclusion, after reading the initial transcripts of this book, my friends, Phil Wolfe and Don Smith, observed that while I professed the importance of affirmation, I was being disingenuous for not articulating my personal beliefs about the business of God. It seemed to me not to be a politically correct thing to do in the context of this whole matter of realizing upon elements leading to personal power; however, the reader may perceive power to be composed of. Whatever God one has faith in is what is important in the context of personal power, so long as the motives are true. One must return from exile in one's own time and place. Yet as I considered their criticism, it struck me that the purpose of the book, which was to provide wisdom and insight into the way that I viewed things in the world for the benefit of Jordan, Brad, and Brian, was that Phil and Don were correct. You need to know what I have faith in. So here it goes, politically correct or not:

I have faith that there is a single presence and power of spirit beyond the physical world that humankind characterizes as God. I have faith that all of humankind is here by the grace of that God, and it is only by recognizing our relationship with spirit that we return to that spiritual source. I have faith that a relationship with spirit is more important than the physical world and what happens around us all in that physical world. I have faith that spirit is in control, not me, although, by my actions and deeds, I manifest the goals of that one presence and power. I have faith that the source of my abundance is from the spirit and that what I receive is because I am an instrument of the spirit. I have faith that being a servant is my duty to humankind and that I must, with humility and solemnity, advance the standard as far on the battlefields of life as my spirit's worldly journey deserves of me. The first step on that journey, each day, is to love others, as Jesus Christ would have loved them. I do my very best every day to not be judgmental, but I do not countenance fools very long. So it is a personal challenge. Lastly, I have faith in those beliefs regardless of the ability to prove or disprove those beliefs in this physical world. That is my spiritual purpose, and I affirm it.

My friend Michael Jamison also reminds me that "faith" and "hope" are two entirely different matters. Hope is based on belief. Faith is based upon knowledge. Hope is "twiddling" your thumbs and wishing in the rocking chair. Faith is acting by the search for truth and the affirmation of the spirit. Walk with faith and affirm your own self-being. Don't stand idly in hope.

The capstone of your pyramid is affirmation.

Your Personal Power Pyramid

I am not bound to win, but I am bound to be true.

I am not bound to succeed, but I am bound to live

up to the light I have.

—Abraham Lincoln

The Eagle

He clasps the crag with crooked hands;
Close to the sun in lonely lands,
Ring'd with the azure world, he stands.

The wrinkled sea beneath him crawls;
He watches from his mountain walls,
And like a thunderbolt, he falls.

—Alfred Tennyson

Chapter 7
Afterthoughts

There have probably been ten million pages written on the issues of self-motivation. There are a thousand and one metaphors or reference points. There are seven reasons, ten reasons, twenty-one reasons, and on and on. Whenever I consider all this wisdom, I am reminded of my friend John Wilhm, who tells the story of the Alcoholics Anonymous organization, working on its principles to be guided by and got to "Rule no. 69." Who could remember the first 68, let alone the first ten? At that point, according to John, the AA founders concluded that maybe they should just follow Rule no. 69, which postulated, "Don't take yourself too seriously." It is in that vein that we should conclude.

Throughout your life, things will happen to you and around you. But events in life, while they may affect you, should never define you. Events only define you if you decide to let them do that. Events only defeat you if you decide to let them do that. How you respond is an important matter. Yes, the events may change the course of your life, but they only destroy you if you decide to let them do that. As I said in the "Introduction," your biography is not your destiny.

I want to leave you with this final observation. In my opinion, all great ideas, great deeds, and great thoughts have humble beginnings. They are often nurtured by pain and by hardship and are likely to be achieved with difficulty. They come about by patience (you know, patience is a virtue. That is why it is so damn hard.)

Great ideas usually come in quiet, meditative moments away from the multitudes of humankind. They speak to us softly, not with a roar. Even if you perceive the great idea, great deed, or great thought as a revelation, it is not. It is the result of your actions, your attitudes, your awareness, your alliances, and your persistent affirmation. It is not winning the lottery. You are in the correct time and place in your spirit's journey through physical space to have it happen.

You have the power to do great things, to think great thoughts, to have great ideas, and to perform great deeds. But you have to do it. And remember that the actions that you take (or don't take) and the choices that you make do matter. Do not become a self-promoter of useless work. You must have a thoughtful purpose.

Would you rather look back on your life and rationalize, "Well, I just could not do it?" Or would you prefer to look back on your life and, in a positive way, say, "Spirit and I did it our way?" Let your spirit have that human journey, and in the end, at the end of the day, you can see how splendid life has been. Most assuredly, you will make mistakes, and there will be other detours that are imposed by external factors in your journey. Often, those are larks that providence has kindly delivered to you anyway. You just have to look for the rainbow. But you have the power to get back on course. You just have to set your mind to do so.

As you move through life, though, do not believe that the burdens of life are solely upon you and you alone. We are all in this together, whether we like it or not. You are not obligated to complete the task of making the world a better place all on your own, but you are likewise not free from your duty to contribute and to participate. The task of making the world a better place cannot be completed in your lifetime. It is never-ending. The task, as I have suggested before, is like the goal of achieving peace. It cannot be stored. It must be continually generated, or the lights go out. The irony of life is that to make a difference, a real difference, requires trust in the goodness of humankind when we know that humankind is doing its very best to extinguish itself daily. In your own small way, you do make a difference. Yet you have to have faith in spirit, and you must recognize that. You must leave something for your God to do. Always remember that the behavior of others, the circumstances of life, cannot take your happiness from you. Only you can do that.

As Master Yoda observed, "Uncertain, the future is." Yet I suggest that the future becomes more certain when you decide to create your own future, and then help create a positive community with others. Don't let the events in the future, the world, or others impose their future on you. That is life by default. Remember that when you take action, the spirit takes action with you, and all of the power comes together to assist you in your journey. Make your own future. You now have a simple and powerful road map that you can refer to on one hand. There are just five simple rules:

1. Act.

2. Have a positive attitude.

3. Cultivate your self-awareness.

4. Create solid alliances.

5. Affirm your spirituality.

And you have the reference point of the greatest, most durable structure ever built by humankind on the earth, the powerful, imposing "Miracle in Stone"—the pyramid. You do not need the twenty-one rules of leaders, the fifteen rules of great salesmen, or the eighteen rules of great "rainmakers." This is all you need, along, of course, with the will and self-discipline to make it happen—to carry the standard the farthest on the field of battle in your lifetime.

Along the way, do not take yourself too seriously. Do not become consumed by work or choked by worldly attachments—stuff. You will not take it with you, and legacies are not made from the fabric of egoism. (I am reminded of the observation, "Eagles may soar, but weasels are not sucked into jet engines!") Be humble.

Edwin Carpenter

Love your God. Smell the flowers. Love someone along the way.
Stop and dance in a puddle, and you will see the rainbow. And when
you have the choice, you might as well dance. The end is
fulfillment—contributions to humankind beyond us.

Keep the faith, and above all, dare to soar! It is your turn to fly.

—Dad (Uncle Ed)

About the Author

Edwin Carpenter is a retired lawyer and business consultant who resides in the nation's heartland near Topeka, Kansas. He has had a long, successful, and interesting career and brings to the reader significant insights into the components of individual success in a simple, fun, and direct manner. The coaching lessons contained in this book will stay with you and remain recurring guideposts for you as you continue your own journey in life, whatever path or paths you may take.

www.ingramcontent.com/pod-product-compliance
Lightning Source LLC
Chambersburg PA
CBHW051214120626
46547CB00013B/1343